The Imagination of Experiences

Aimed at lay, student, and academic readers alike, this book concerns the imagination and, specifically, imagination in music. It opens with a discussion of the invalidity of the idea of the creative genius and the connected view that ideas originate just in the individual mind. An alternative view of the imaginative process is then presented, that ideas spring from a subconscious dialogue activated by engagement in the world around. Ideas are therefore never just of our own making. This view is supported by evidence from many studies and corresponds with descriptions by artists of their experience of imagining. The third subject is how imaginations can be shared when musicians work with other artists, and the way the constraints imposed by trying to share subconscious imagining result in clearly distinct forms of joint working. The final chapter covers the use of the musical imagination in making meanings from music. The evidence is that music does not communicate meanings directly, and so composers or performers cannot be looked to as authorities on its meaning. Instead, music is commonly heard as analogous to human experience, and listeners who perceive such analogies may then imagine their own meanings from the music.

After a career as a geography academic, civil servant, local government officer, and political activist, Alan Taylor turned to music halfway through life and has since gained a PhD on the subject of the musical imagination. He is an active community musician, conducting two ensembles, performing in others, and directing the Herne Hill Music Festival.

The Imagination of Experiences
Musical Invention, Collaboration, and the Making of Meanings

Alan Taylor

LONDON AND NEW YORK

First published 2021
by Routledge
2 Park Square, Milton Park, Abingdon, Oxon OX14 4RN

and by Routledge
605 Third Avenue, New York, NY 10017

Routledge is an imprint of the Taylor & Francis Group, an Informa business

Copyright © 2021 Alan Taylor

The right of Alan Taylor to be identified as author of this work has been asserted by him in accordance with sections 77 and 78 of the Copyright, Designs and Patents Act 1988.

All rights reserved. No part of this book may be reprinted or reproduced or utilised in any form or by any electronic, mechanical, or other means, now known or hereafter invented, including photocopying and recording, or in any information storage or retrieval system, without permission in writing from the publishers.

Trademark notice: Product or corporate names may be trademarks or registered trademarks and are used only for identification and explanation without intent to infringe.

British Library Cataloguing-in-Publication Data
A catalogue record for this book is available from the British Library

Library of Congress Cataloging-in-Publication Data
A catalog record has been requested for this book

ISBN 13: 978-0-367-56928-0 (hbk)

Typeset in Times New Roman
by Newgen Publishing UK

Contents

Acknowledgements   vii

Introduction   1
The subjects covered in the book 3
How the subjects are tackled 4

1   **The redundant genius, who won't lie down and die**   6
Introduction 6
The last refuge of the scoundrel genius 6
Bach didn't write musical works 12
Why the scoundrel won't just lie down and die 15
Conclusion 19

2   **The musical imagination as dialogue**   25
Introduction 25
Part 1: Theory 26
Part 2: Accounts by composers (and others) 40
Conclusion 47

3   **Sharing imaginations**   54
Introduction 54
The misuse of the term 'collaboration' 55
*Going back to first principles – four types of working
    relationships 59*
Are there intermediate types of working? 61
The experience of different types of working 66
The need for a language of communication 67
Conclusion 71

4 Making musical meanings: the imaginative listener 75
Introduction 75
Part 1: The sources of meaning in music 76
Part 2: How the sense of musical meaning may arise 86
Conclusion 99

A final word 107
Index 112

Acknowledgements

I would like to thank Professors Paul Barker and Maria Delgado for the stimulus provided by their research supervision when I was studying at the Central School of Speech and Drama, and also the many friends and family members who read and commented on sections of this book, especially Rachel Wicking, Derek Taylor, Jenni Pinnock, Litha Efthymiou, and Janet Oates. I would also like to thank the various pre-publication reviewers of the book for their helpful comments and suggestions.

Introduction

How ideas are imagined; how people share imaginative work; how they imagine meanings from experiences. Those are the three subjects of this book, and I explore them in relation to music.

Music is an excellent subject for the study of the imagination. It is the result of imaginative work and is widely experienced as meaningful by those who hear it. Yet it is hard to define what music communicates since the sounds do not stand for anything outside of themselves. This makes it is easier to focus on the process of the musical imagination rather than its results.

The imagination appears to be used in much the same way in all musical activities. As Hargreaves, Hargreaves, and North put it '… there is a clear consensus [among academic researchers] … that common mental structures underlie the three main activities of invention (composing and improvising), performance, and listening.' (2012, 162). A composer imagines sounds and chooses and develops those which please and seem meaningful to them. A performer, reading notation, imagines a meaningful flow to the music and performs this rather than just the written notes. A listener, hearing musical ideas and structures, seeks to imagine a sense of meaning in them. As Olivetti Belardinelli puts it, in each of these activities a person uses their imagination to '… transmit information into the interior … in a way that reduces its entropy.' (2006, 327); that is, they seek to reduce the perceived disorder or complexity in the music by imagining a sense of meaning to bring order to the experience.

I suggest a way of looking at each of my three subjects: how music is invented, with the focus on composing (Chapters 1 & 2), how this process of imagining music can be shared (Chapter 3), and how listeners imagine meanings from the experience of music (Chapter 4). My approach in each case is to review the arguments and evidence presented by many other writers on how the musical imagination works, a concentrated form of analysis which I have not seen published previously. Working through so many and varied studies led me to suggest new ideas on each subject, ideas which I hope will take the understanding of each subject a few steps forward.

Since I've used the term 'imagination' in my title, one question worth addressing at this point is whether there is any difference between this and creativity. Hargreaves, Miell, and MacDonald suggest that imagination is about perception, about seeing something potentially new, while creativity concerns doing, about making something which may be new (2012, 3). Since my aim is to examine how people come up with ideas, rather than what they make with them, I will follow their definitions and use the term 'imagination' throughout. However, I doubt whether a hard-and-fast distinction can be drawn between the two since they shade into one another in practice, even if defined in these ways.

One of my aims is to counter the widespread impression that musical imagination is a mysterious ability possessed mainly by exceptional people. There is extensive evidence on how people come up with ideas, and this does not support the view that they simply emerge from the imagination working in isolation, or that this ability is limited to particular people. Rather, ideas result from every person's interaction with their environment and are then worked on until they feel just right. The result, as Sawyer points out, is that art is not the result of '… inspiration from a lone genius …' Instead, it results from '… hard work peppered with mini-insights, and these mini-insights don't seem that mysterious in the context of the preceding work.' (2006, 159).

Yet there does remain a mysterious element to imagining in the arts since artists have commented that they cannot explain what they imagine. For example, painter Frank Auerbach commented that painting is '… something that happens to a man working in a room, alone with his actions, his ideas, and perhaps his model.' (2018). While Auerbach was aware that he was the person whose actions resulted in the art, he felt that the paintings happened through him but were not his conscious creations.

The question, then, is how to study the operation of the imagination when artists have rarely described where their ideas come from and may be unable to do so. However, artists have often described their experience of imagining. These descriptions can be brought together with the many studies of the underlying processes to shed light on the way the imagination works.

The views I suggest apply to music, and most of my examples and studies concern music, and specifically Western Art Music.[1] However, I do quote relevant statements by other artists, and it is possible that the suggestions I put forward may apply more widely. I will leave that to readers to decide for themselves.

The subjects covered in the book

In Chapter 1 I examine the enduring stereotype of the 'genius' composer, seen as an exceptional person able to summon great music from the depths of their imagination. The genius idea has been roundly attacked in recent years as inconsistent with the evidence of how music is written. It is linked to the concept of the 'musical work', seen as an expression of the composer's intentions. Both ideas arose in the historical circumstances around 1800 and reflect the values and economic situation of that time. However, the genius idea has persisted since then because it is a widely-believed ideology which influences how people see artists. There are also aspects of our thinking process which may reinforce the idea by leading people to imagine that ideas arise just from the working of their own minds.

In Chapter 2 I look at the evidence on how the imagination in fact works. Drawing on the findings and arguments of writers on aesthetics, psychology, and neurology I suggest that the imagination has three key characteristics: ideas emerge from a dialogue between influences a person has absorbed; these influences are the result of active engagement in both the society around us and our wider environment; and the imagination operates largely subconsciously, with ideas then just popping into the conscious mind. This subconscious process depends on our embodied engagement with the world around us, rather than operating just within our minds.

I then look at descriptions by composers and other artists of their experience of imaginative work. These correspond with the view I suggest of how the imagination works and also show that artists imagine in the language of their art form. As well, they point to there being two separate activities which make up the imaginative process: imagining ideas and evaluating them.

This last conclusion is central to my discussion of artistic 'collaboration' in Chapter 3. Artists who work together need to be able to share their imaginative processes, and that means being able to share imagining and evaluating ideas. The way they work together will depend on which of these two essentially subconscious activities they are able to share; one, the other, neither, or both. Since not all groups of artists will find they can share both of these activities within the imaginative process, there must be a series of distinct ways of sharing such work.

Moving on to imagination in listening, if composers are geniuses then it would seem natural to look to them to try to understand the meaning of their music. The statement in that sentence is packed with implications and assumptions which, frankly, need to be unpacked. The first thing which needs to be examined is how meanings are made from music, and the second concerns who makes them. Another issue is the meaning of the word 'meaning' when we are talking about music.

This is the subject of Chapter 4. The view I suggest in Chapter 2 of how the imagination works is central to this since the implication is that a musician will be no better qualified than anyone else to explain their music. Their ideas arise from a subconscious dialogue between influences of which they may not be fully aware, and so nothing they say about the meaning of their music can be taken as definitive.

The question, then, is how and why listeners feel music to be meaningful. My suggestion is that they use their subconscious imaginations to create meanings from the experience of the music, rather than musical meanings being communicated directly. The evidence is that their engagement in music may lead them to sense it as meaningful because it seems analogous to human experience. Listeners may then try to define these meanings by seeking parallels with their own experiences or with those they can imagine.

How the subjects are tackled

My aim is to offer readers a concentrated and comprehensive survey of research on the musical imagination of a type not previously available. My approach to each subject is to work through the published arguments and studies and then to suggest a new view which goes a little beyond existing positions. I show that each of these new views is consistent with descriptions of the experience of imagining music. Each chapter consists of a careful progression through the evidence and arguments to arrive at this new conclusion.

The book is aimed at lay, student, and academic readers alike, and the style of the writing is influenced by there being this wide range of potential readers. I have aimed to write in readily-comprehensible language, though I have followed academic conventions in the writing, principally by including references to the many sources I quote. Readers who wish to follow up any of these then can, while others may just skip them. I have also followed the academic convention of referring to other writers in the present tense, though it seemed artificial to continue this practice back before 1940.

Each reader will experience my arguments in their own way and make their own meanings from them. This brings me back to my title, which sums up the view I have of music or any other art for that matter. Musicians imagine experiences to offer to audiences, and these grow out of the musician's own accumulated experience. Each member of their audience, on encountering the music, may imagine their own meanings from the experience. As Dewey argues, art does not consist so much of works as of their experiencing (2005, 1).

Note

1 Western Art Music is a widely-used term for the music which emerged mainly from the medieval Catholic Church and early European aristocratic courts and which continues to the present day. It usually involves a separation of the roles of composer, performers, and audience.

References

Auerbach, Frank. 2018. "Auerbach Comes to New York at Timothy Taylor." *Art Market Monitor*. Accessed 12 August 2018. www.artmarketmonitor.com/2018/05/08/82461/

Dewey, John. 2005. *Art as Experience*. New York. The Berkley Publishing Group.

Hargreaves, David J., James J. Hargreaves, & Adrian C. North. 2012. "Imagination and Creativity in Listening." In *Musical Imaginations: Multidisciplinary Perspectives on Creativity, Performance, and Perception*, edited by David J. Hargreaves, Dorothy E. Miell & Raymond A.R. MacDonald, 156–72. Oxford: Oxford University Press. DOI: 10.1093/acprof:oso/9780199568086.001.0001

Hargreaves, David J., Dorothy E. Miell, & Raymond A.R. MacDonald. 2012. *Musical Imaginations: Multidisciplinary Perspectives on Creativity, Performance, and Perception*. Oxford & New York: Oxford University Press. DOI: 10.1093/acprof:oso/9780199568086.001.0001

Sawyer, Keith. 2006. *Explaining Creativity: The Science of Human Innovation*. Oxford & New York: Oxford University Press.

1 The redundant genius, who won't lie down and die

Introduction

And so, to knock down the idea of the genius composer yet again when it has been so discredited by modern research? Such an exercise might seem pointless after the demolition jobs by Clarke and Doffman (2017) and Cook (2018) in their recent books. However, the view of imagination as a characteristic just of special individuals still has a powerful hold over the way musicians are seen. I therefore don't think it would be credible to propose an alternative, as I do in Chapter 2, without first explaining why the genius myth is based on an inaccurate view of the imagination.

I start by looking at the arguments of writers who show that the genius concept, and the idea of the musical 'work' to which it is linked, do not fit with the evidence of how musicians imagine and how music is made and performed. An important alternative view has been proposed called 'distributed creativity', which is supported by evidence that music always depends on the creative contributions of many people rather than just a few exceptional individuals. I follow this with a critique of the concept of the musical work, seen as the creation of composers working alone.

I then examine the nature of the genius myth as an ideology which influences both audiences and the self-perception of musicians. Evidence contrary to ideologies such as this may be resisted or rejected by those who believe in them. There are also aspects of how the imagination works which can lead artists to think that ideas arise just from their own minds. This is an illusion, but it is one which can make it harder to shake oneself free from the ideology of the lone creator.

The last refuge of the scoundrel genius[1]

Western Art Music is described by Sawyer as '... the one remaining bastion of the solitary lone genius myth.' (2014, 285). It is certainly my impression, as a back-row viola player in my local symphony orchestra,[2] that most of my colleagues and our audience see the famous composers whose music we perform in this way, but the evidence is that this view does not correspond with the nature of compositional work.

The work of composition

The idea of the composer genius has been roundly criticised in academic writing, for instance by Hayden and Windsor who describe the erroneous view of '… an isolated, possibly unhinged, genius, struggling at the piano or desk.' (2007, 28) and Harley who writes of the '… nineteenth-century image of the wilful composer creating music in tortured but inspired isolation …' (2008, 129). I have nothing to add to or take away from the arguments of these writers, or those I mentioned at the start of the chapter, and so it is best to summarise the main elements of their case as I see them:

1. The creativity required to produce music does not just come from a limited number of people, the composers. Music, like all art, results from the direct or indirect creative contributions of many people, extending beyond composers and performers to those who have influenced them and those in the past who contributed to the evolution of each style of music and performance. The term 'art world' is used by Becker (2008) for this constellation of people. He studied how a wide variety of pieces of art were made and found in every case that their making depended on many people. He concludes that 'Every art, then, rests on an extensive division of labour.' (2008, 13). The same view has been put forward by Sawyer and DeZutter (2009), Clarke and Doffman (2017), and Cook (2018), and termed 'distributed creativity' on the grounds that art depends on the creative contributions of many people.
2. Even in the part of the process called composition, the evidence from sketches, manuscripts, and accounts by composers is that their work consists mostly of the painstaking application of craft skills. In a sense, anyone can make up a tune or motif, but it takes great skill, and skill which can be learned and practised, to make something of it. Written evidence of composers imagining music complete and then just writing it down, as Sawyer (2006, 225) and Cook (2018, 96–108) note, has been shown to consist of forgeries created to propagate the idea of the spontaneous genius. The reality is that composition consists mostly of hard work.

It might be objected that, even though a great deal of work is required to complete a composition, the genius composer is a person who can invent remarkable musical ideas to start with. However, much of the greatest music is based on simple ideas, such as the four-note motif which Beethoven used for most of the first movement of his 5th Symphony. It may take a composer a great deal of work to arrive at exactly the right version of a musical idea after an initial thought, and they apply their craft skills until they happen on a version which satisfies them. We know that Beethoven repeatedly sketched ideas before choosing a version he was happy with, for instance making more than two hundred sketches before settling on the theme of the *Ode to Joy* (Konečni 2012, 148). His distinctiveness consisted of working hard till an idea was just right, rather than in the brilliance of his initial inventions.

3. Composers have always worked with other artists, and have been stimulated by their input, rather than imagining music on their own. The historical record is full of examples of composers showing drafts to other people, asking their opinion, and making changes, as I will show in Chapter 3. Creativity in art, as Novitz argues, is often '… the result of interaction between minds, not the result of a single mind working in isolation.' (Novitz 2003, 189).

4. Composers always work within artistic traditions and draw on pre-existing styles and approaches. As Carroll points out, the judgement that an artist is exceptional is not based just on their personal abilities, but on '… how the art work behaves against the background of tradition.' (2003, 231). He sees the dependence of artists on the traditions they have inherited as inconsistent with the idea of that '… godlike individualism …' (2003, 211) which is the essence of the idea of the creative genius. Even when a composer makes an apparently revolutionary break, this can be seen to grow out of previous developments. For example, Schoenberg came up with the radical idea of a 12-tone series, and this enabled him to overcome the creative block he experienced after his participation in the First World War. This technique may seem like a complete break from previous styles based on musical keys but it in fact developed from the increasingly chromatic style of his previous music, which had already become almost detached from musical keys. As Adolfe shows, he was writing virtual 12-tone music before he invented the theory (2001, 80). Schoenberg saw 12-tone technique as a natural development in his work and denied that he was a revolutionary (Schoenberg 1975, 137).

5. We know that composers were responsive to their social and political environments, rather than writing as solitary individuals with no context. For example, in his book *Mozart and the Enlightenment* (1992), Till describes the arrival of freemasonry in Vienna, the increasing involvement of the bourgeois and progressive aristocrats in the movement, its relationship to the reforming monarchy of the time, and Mozart's involvement and eventual decision to join a lodge of specifically Catholic masons (1992, 117–29). He describes how Mozart was deeply engaged in contemporaneous social movements and ideas and links the development of his music to the evolution of his thinking within the context of freemasonry, Catholicism, and absolute monarchy. Similarly, McClary describes Bach's relationship to the intellectual and artistic currents of his time, explaining that he was an outsider as a German in a society which had been culturally colonised by the musical styles of Italian opera and French absolutism. He drew on both sources in developing his music but, she argues, he '… chose to maintain his marginalized position, to appropriate all available musical discourses while clinging fiercely to his own German heritage, and to forge perhaps not so much a unified tonality as a set of eclectic hybrids.' (1987, 20).

None of this, it should not need saying, takes away from the fact that the best-known composers were highly skilled, or that their pieces are remarkable achievements. However, we should see their music as having been written within a context, with its creation and character directly and indirectly influenced by their involvement with the society and people around them, and by others in the past. Their pieces are not timeless masterworks created by geniuses who cannot be questioned, but historically-situated art which we can appreciate more fully through a better understanding of its context.

I hope that I have said enough to show that the genius myth does not fit with the evidence on how composers imagine. The findings of research on two further subjects are also inconsistent with the idea of the composer genius. These are:

- Distributed creativity, mentioned at the start – the view that music always requires the creative contributions of many people.
- The concept of the musical work, seen as the expression of the composer's imagination.

Distributed musical creativity

This term is used by Sawyer and DeZutter (2009), Clarke and Doffman (2017), and Cook (2018) for the view that music, and other art, results from the direct or indirect creative contributions of many people rather than just a few creative geniuses. As an example, Brahms wrote his *Violin Concerto in D Major, Op. 77* while working closely with its first soloist, Joachim. Both of them were working within a tradition which had evolved through the contributions of many others. Schwarz (1983) describes how Brahms wrote with Joachim's performing style in mind, consulted him in detail on passages, accepted or responded to his suggested changes, and made further alterations after the first performance. There have been many similar studies of artists working together, for instance by John-Steiner in her classic book *Creative Collaboration* (2000). In recent years, numerous studies have been published of composers and other artists working together on new pieces.[3] The pieces were not created by the composers alone, or even by composers supported by others who had merely functional roles. In every case, the composers worked closely with their artistic partners, and within traditions and idioms to which many people had contributed, with performances requiring the creative contributions of further people to bring the music to life.

This area of study has been taken forward in a series of books from the Centre for Musical Performance as Creative Practice (CMPCP). The first that is relevant here is *Beyond the Score* by Cook (2013). He explains how the study of music has focussed on written scores as the expression of the composer's intentions, and so music has been presented as if it were a text-based art produced just by composers. By contrast, the experience of music is that it is what is heard rather than written. Cook examines a wide range of examples which illustrate his argument that, even for music performed from detailed notation, the printed notes are not the same as the experience of the music. It follows from this that music as heard depends on the creative contributions of many people.

Earlier, Sawyer and DeZutter (2009) described how research on creativity initially focussed on identifying the characteristics of creative individuals, but how attention shifted by the 1980s to the study of collaborative creative relationships (2009, 81–2). Their own study was of five improvisatory theatre performances, and they describe the creative process as 'distributed' since it was one '… where collaborating groups of individuals collectively generate a shared creative product.' (2009, 82). In other words, they present creativity as capable of arising from the interaction between artists working together directly.

A second book in the CMPCP series, *Distributed Creativity* by Clarke and Doffman (2017), consists of a series of studies which illustrate how music results from a process influenced by or involving a variety of people. The editors describe the '… increasing recognition of the extended and distributed character of music's creative process.' (2017, 2). Taken together, the contributions in the book add up to a convincing case that music usually results from creative inputs by many people, each influenced by their wider environment. In the final book in the CMPCP series, Cook (2018) takes the discussion on distributed creativity further. In his first full chapter (2018, 15–68), he argues from a wide range of examples that music always depends on the creative contributions of many people.

The same argument, that imagination depends on human interconnectedness and interaction, has been put forward frequently in recent years. Toynbee (2017) suggests that we should see music-making as work rather than the endless innovation of new sounds, and that this points to a distributed view of creativity since work is inescapably the result of collective endeavour. As the psychologists Sloman and Fernbach put it, 'When you put it all together, human thought is incredibly impressive. But it is a product of community, not of the individual alone.' (2011, 5). The same conclusion is reached by Beard in his survey of the most effective educational systems in the world. He quotes the CEO of a Californian high school as saying that 'Knowledge is not something that individuals do by themselves, but something we do together.' (Beard 2017, 275).

The development of this now widely-accepted view represents a step forward in our understanding of the process of music creation. However, this view seems to me to be incomplete since it does not include an explanation of how individuals come up with ideas to contribute to making music. This point is made by Lindon and Clarke (2017) in the book edited by Clarke and Doffman. The authors note that, while ideas result from the interaction between many people and their norms and traditions (2017, 55), even so, '… cognition must originate in the mind of the individual (after all, our thoughts, insights and new discoveries seem to occur in our own heads) …' (2017, 54). This is the reason I suggest that the concept of distributed creativity offers an incomplete basis for understanding the making of art. It does not cover the part of the process which takes place within the individual's imagination.

The studies quoted in this section show that music results from the direct or indirect contributions of many people, and that creativity does not reside just with a few genius composers. We may, as a result, be halfway towards a modern view of the musical imagination as an alternative to the essentially nineteenth-century idea of the composer genius. This half-alternative concerns influences on the musical imagination from outside the individual mind and the way people then combine to make music. It needs to be complemented by a view of how individuals imagine musical ideas and understandings, which is the subject of Chapter 2.

Bach didn't write musical works

A widely-held view of Western Art Music is that it consists of works and that the composers are their creators. As Kanga puts it:

> The concept of the 'work' is one of the central myths of music. In conventional and popular usage, the work, created by a sole (genius) author, the composer, endures as a score that is then interpreted by performers.
>
> (2014, 155)

The work concept does not fit with the evidence examined in the previous section on the way composers write and the many creative contributions required to make music. It has also been challenged on two other grounds:

1. That it arose at a specific point in musical history and may not apply to music of other periods.
2. That it does not correspond with the reality of music in performance.

History

In her analysis of the work concept, Goehr argues that it only became fully established around 1800 and so should not be applied to earlier music such as Bach's. As an example of this new view, she quotes Beethoven, in a letter to his publisher, commenting on more detailed specifications in scores such as metronome marks in addition to markings such as *Allegro*, and explaining that '... the performers must now obey the ideas of the unfettered genius.' (1992, 225). Beethoven was not only asserting his right to specify the tempo exactly but also, by using the word 'now', recognising that this was a new attitude.

Before the late Eighteenth Century, as Goehr shows (1992, 176–204), written music was regarded less as a fixed set of unique works and more as material produced for specific circumstances or events, and which could be re-used, borrowed, or stolen. Judging from the letter quoted above, Beethoven was concerned to maintain control over performances in a way which reflected a different view of his scores to that of earlier composers.

This view is questioned by Trillo (2019), who mentions the example of Opus (work) numbers given by composers to some of their pieces by the late Seventeenth Century onwards (2019, 35). However, he agrees with Goehr that the view of musical works did change around 1800, with a shift away from music being seen as the result of skilled performance and towards performance being seen as replication of the score (Trillo 2019, 28), and that earlier composers generally saw their music differently from how it is now often regarded, as enduring works. As Small explains, Mozart did not compose his pieces for '… the kind of abstract contemplation to which we subject them today but as actively participant elements in the social and religious rituals of his time.' (1998, 107).

Without wanting to attribute this new aesthetic attitude only to changes in the economics of composition, it did develop alongside new ways in which composers could earn money. These meant that composers could present themselves, and be seen, as independent artists rather than principally as craftspeople employed by the Church and aristocracy. For instance, public concert halls to accommodate the growing bourgeois audience began to be constructed, giving composers greater opportunities to earn through the performance. The earliest public concert hall in Vienna, the Theater an der Wein, was built in 1801 and hosted the premieres of many of Beethoven's orchestral pieces.

The development of this new view of composers as artists was also linked to changes in legal rights over the publication of music. Attali (1985) argues that the development of copyright law during this period offered composers scope, for the first time, to earn through the sale of sheet music, partly to meet the demand from the new bourgeois public for music to play at home. In her study of the development of legal rights of composers over their notation, Barron quotes a judgement in favour of J.C. Bach in his case against a music publisher, which established Bach's rights over his notation (2006, 118), and explains how the resulting:

> capacity to earn a living by selling one's works in the market freed the artist of the burden of pleasing the patron; the only requirement now was to please the buying public.
>
> (2006, 123)

These changes happened at the same time as the development of the idea that music was separate from its social context, as Goehr shows in her essay *On the Politics of Musical Interpretation* (1993). Before the late Eighteenth Century, theorists saw music as contributing to society, with musical meaning connected closely to the social context of the performance (1993, 180–1). Later composers, by contrast, wished to be treated as autonomous artists and saw their music as separate from society to a greater extent (1993, 183).

There was clearly a significant change in composers' attitudes around 1800, even though some earlier composers saw their music in ways close to the one which became predominant from the early Nineteenth Century.[4] It is this new view of composers as autonomous artists, and of music as separate from society, which Attali considers was made possible by changes such as the establishment of copyright laws. As he puts it 'The artist was born at the same time as his work went on sale.' (1985, 47).

The result was the establishment of the idea that music consisted of 'works' created by composers from their imaginations alone. While there is limited evidence that music was imagined in new ways, composers began to regard their music differently due to the greater freedom permitted by the changing intellectual and economic environment. They came to see their imagination as operating alone, to some extent at least, because they no longer had to write primarily to please aristocratic or ecclesiastical patrons or employers. Since these ideas developed in the historical circumstances around 1800, they do not apply fully to earlier music and are not necessarily of continuing relevance.

Performance

The second line of attack, so to speak, on the work concept comes from writers on performance, who show that it is inaccurate to think of musical works as fixed objects defined by the composer since this does not correspond with the experience of music in performance. Bowen argues that pieces of music change their character through time as performance practice changes. He shows, for instance, that Mahler's *Symphony No. 6 in A minor*, one of his many examples, has become longer on average as time has passed because conductors have come to take it more slowly (1993, 164–5).

Further examples of how the perceived meaning of pieces of music changes over time as performers come to interpret them differently are described by Leech-Wilkinson. He describes how the view of Schubert as a naïve lyricist changed to one of a composer with more troubled depths, due in particular to the performances by Fischer-Diskau of the composer's song-cycles (2012, 2). He writes that '... what a piece of music is and what it means depends on when and where it is made by performers and experienced by listeners ...' (2012, 7). He therefore questions the idea that the meaning resides in the score and originates with the composer. He sees the idea of the musical work as one which may exist in composers' minds but which does not reflect the evolving nature of music in performance (2012, 10).

A detailed study of his own relationship as a performer to pieces of music, and their status as works, was carried out by Östersjö (2008). He proposes a '... model in which the identity of the musical work is analysed as the result of interaction between multiple agents: composer, performer, instrument, score and electronics, among others.' (2008, 1). If this is the case, then the idea of a musical work as a stable concept related just to the score and the composer is misleading since the character of the piece will change with changing performance practice. Specifically, Östersjö questions the work concept in its application to contemporary music since there is no generally known performance tradition (2008, 20).

Music, rather than being conceived as an ideal object embodied by the score, should therefore be seen only as performances, and these will inevitably differ from one another. As Cook points out:

> Many of Chopin's and Liszt's works survive in any number of different, equally authentic notated versions, themselves the traces of different, equally authentic performances.
>
> (2001, 10)

It is, then, widely accepted that the idea of the musical work only came to dominate composers' thinking consistently from 1800. This was linked to the development of new aesthetic ideas about the role of artists as independent creators, which combined with composers' growing ability to earn an independent living to alter perceptions of the process of composition. This new (in 1800) view of musical works as created by genius composers is not consistent either with the evidence of distributed nature of creativity or with the reality of the changing nature of pieces in performance.

Why the scoundrel won't just lie down and die

Nevertheless, the idea that composers are genius creators is still widely believed and at times seems to resist both evidence and argument. One of the reasons for this is the status of the genius myth as an ideology. The other concerns the mental processes through which ideas emerge.

Ideology

It is one thing to present arguments and evidence to demonstrate that an idea is invalid. It is quite another to change people's minds and persuade them of a more soundly based view. This is especially true if the problematic idea acts as an ideology; that is, a concept which shapes how people perceive experience. Belief in an ideology can lead people to resist evidence which contradicts their fixed view.

Evidence that the genius idea is an ideology is found in how the way the concept is understood has changed through history. Guyer (2003) shows how philosophers such as Kant, Emerson, and J.S. Mill defined the idea in different ways which were influenced by, and influenced, thinking at the time. In this way, he shows that the genius idea is an interpretation or a concept rather than a fact, and one which has changed as the intellectual and aesthetic environment of which it forms a part has changed.

While this ideology emerged over 200 years ago, it still influences attitudes today. Goehr describes how, in the early Nineteenth Century:

> Musicians began to think about music as involving creation, performance, and reception not just as music *per se*, but of works as such. The concept of the work first began to serve musical practice in its regulative capacity at this time.
>
> (1992, x)

The key idea here is that the work concept 'regulates' – that is controls – how audiences perceive Western Art Music. Goehr writes of '... the lack of ability we presently seem to have to speak about music in any other way [than as works].' (1992, 243). Similarly, Lucas sees the musical work and the idea of the genius composer as combining to form the '... ideology of western art music, [in which] the composer has been privileged as an autonomous author, and hence the owner of a 'work'...' (Lucas 2016, 186).

Since concert programmes of Western Art Music still consist mainly of pieces written when the idea of the musical work was dominant, it is not surprising that it still influences composers, even though the historical circumstances have changed radically. Hankinson and O'Grady suggest that there are modern composers who, influenced by this ideology, regard their scores as the embodiment of their music, writing that:

> The stated ideology of many composers may still be that the aesthetic quality of the composition as notated, its *potential* for performance, is the main issue. [i.e. the main concern of the composer]
> (1981, 31)

The ideology of the solitary creator or genius has also been criticised on two other grounds, first because it can act as a barrier to collaborative working, and second for being a gender-based stereotype.

Modern composers frequently work with musical performers or other artists when composing, and problems can result if the composer sees themselves as the sole creator of their music. They may, as a result, be reluctant to share the creative process and have a fixed view of their musical language, which acts as a barrier to accepting creative input from a performer. Three performers who studied their own collaborations with composers, Roche (2011, 19–20), Roe (2007, 1), and Harrison (2012, 212–17 & 218–25), encountered this problem. Similarly, Hayden and Windsor argue that composers who see themselves as lone creators of musical works may resist sharing control over the creative process (1981, 31).

On the second point, Redhead (2016) criticises the genius-composer concept as gender-based. She comments that the cult of the genius does not fit '... the figure of the composer as craftsperson as found in women's discourse [and is] an historical narrative [which] has a male psychological profile.' (2016, 174). Glazner, commenting on literary art, writes in the same vein of the need to replace '... the patriarchal account of individualistic literary creation with a politicised account of the social production of literature.' (2001, 155).

The concept of the creative genius has been reinforced in recent years by its closeness to the idea which Toynbee calls the 'ideology of creativity' (IOC), in which creativity is seen just as a characteristic of individuals rather than the outcome of work, and work which of necessity involves and depends on other people (Toynbee 2017, 38). He links this to the imperatives of the modern market economy, writing that the '... cultural industries, including the music industry, use the IOC to help create markets.' (2017, 39), Music makers are as a result encouraged to present themselves as unique creators competing for attention and work. The same point is made by Cook, who attacks what he sees as the hijacking of the idea of creativity to support the neo-liberal ideology within which creativity is seen as a means of generating novelties (2018, 197).

However, the enduring power of the genius idea, combined with the neo-liberal ideology of artists as individuals competing, can make it hard to convince some people that musical imagination is not only an ability possessed by exceptional individuals. The fact is, we all have the potential to imagine and invent, even though most people in Western cultures do not develop this capacity fully. Picasso was closer to the truth when he said that 'Every child is an artist. The problem is how to remain an artist once we grow up.' (2016).

Mental processes

The neurological processes which operate as we imagine can lead to the mental illusion that ideas originate just in our own imaginations. Since ideas seem to simply 'appear' in our own heads, it is easy to fall into thinking that their source must be just our own mental processes. This can act as a further barrier to accepting the evidence that imaginative work depends on influences which each person has absorbed, and therefore is inextricably bound up with the person's environment. Unless a composer is sufficiently self-aware, there is a risk that this potential illusion may lead them to think that they alone are the source of their ideas.

I deal with the way in which ideas emerge more fully in Chapter 2, but it is important here to outline the neurological processes which underlie subconscious and conscious thought, and how these can result in the impression that ideas have come simply from within our own minds. This question is examined by neuroscientists Kounios and Beeman (2015), who studied the brain activity which takes place before and at the moment an idea occurs to a person. They show that ideas appear first in the subconscious mind, with brain areas associated with subconscious thought lighting up first, followed by areas associated with conscious thought when the person becomes aware of them (2015, 86). As a result, a person may think that they have just come up with an idea when in fact it had already been developing in their subconscious. They describe, as an example, hearing an idea from another person, forgetting it, and then the idea returning. A person may then have the illusion that the idea must have arisen from their own mental activity. They describe the sense that 'If it came all of a sudden, then it must be my idea!' (2015, 104).

This same question is examined by Wiggins, who argues that composers may be misled in their perception of their imaginative process due to its reliance on subconscious thought. He explains how '… an idea appears in consciousness without warning, and without any indication of whence it came.' (2012, 306) and so can be perceived by the person concerned as just of their own invention.

As Kounios and Beeman explain, '… the aha moment [when we have an idea] occurs when an idea that's already slightly activated in the right hemisphere [of the brain] – but is still unconscious – suddenly emerges into awareness as an insight.' (2015, 80).

Konečni draws the same conclusion from his review of a wide range of experiences of imagining, and notes studies showing spikes in brain activity prior to an insight (2012, 144). Rather than appearing as if from nowhere, the tracking of this process shows that ideas in fact emerge into our conscious minds after a peak in subconscious activity. As well, examples from composers which I quote in Chapter 2 suggest that this peak is preceded by a longer subconscious process, often taking place during periods of relaxation or distraction.

In Chapter 2 I discuss the evidence that ideas are provoked in this way by engagement with external stimuli, and how they emerge from a subconscious dialogue between many influences. Everybody absorbs many ideas and learns many things which affect their thinking, conscious and subconscious. When subconscious mental activity subsequently leads to the appearance of an idea in the conscious mind, this process will have been affected by our experiences and the way in which we have learned from these. In other words, ideas are never just our own.

However, since it is impossible to be fully aware of one's own imaginative process, people may suffer from the illusion that ideas come from their imaginations alone. This can reinforce the perception of lone creation and the view of the composer as the sole source of creative input into making music.

Conclusion

The idea, and self-perception, of composers as artists who write musical works, developed around 1800 and is reflected by Beethoven's self-description as an '… unfettered genius.' (Goehr 1992, 225). The concept did not, and does not, reflect the reality of the imaginative process in composition, or the many influences on, and contributions to, the creation of music. As well, the experience of composed music in performance does not correspond to the idea of musical works made by composers alone.

Nevertheless, the genius idea remains powerful due to its character as an ideology which influences how people perceive music and composers.

Its roots lie in the changed circumstances around 1800 which helped the ideology to become established, and in the illusion of lone creation which may result from the sudden appearance of ideas in the conscious mind. Its power has been reinforced recently by the neo-liberal view of artists as separate and competing individuals.

An alternative to this view could be based on the concept of creativity as distributed, combined with the more soundly-based view of the way the individual imagination works which I suggest in Chapter 2. However, to win wide acceptance, any alternative view would need to contend with the enduring power of the genius ideology and the reasons for this endurance.

Notes

1 With apologies to Dr Samuel Johnson, quoted by Boswell as saying that 'Patriotism is the last refuge of the scoundrel.' (Johnson 2016)
2 Dulwich Symphony Orchestra, London. dulwichsymphonyorchestra.org.uk
3 Examples of collaborative working by composers are described by Fitch and Heyde (2007), Harley (2008), Hayden & Windsor (2007), Hastings (1983), Jordan (2000), Stiefel (2006), Bennett (2012), Casey (2016), Styles (2016), Crimp & Benjamin (2014), Watts (2010), Gorton and Östersjö (2016), Aslan and Lloyd (2016), and in PhD theses by Roe (2007), Roche (2011), Harrison (2012), and Kanga (2014).
4 See the arguments of White (1997) and Butt (2018) that some Baroque composers regarded their music in ways similar to the work concept. White accepts that his view is a qualification of Goehr's analysis.

References

Adolfe, Bruce. 2001. "With Music in Mind." In *The Origin of Creativity*, edited by Karl H. Pfenninger & Valerie R. Shubik, 69–88. Oxford & New York: Oxford University Press. DOI: 10.1093/acprof:oso/9780199836963.001.0001

Aslan, Jessica & Emma Lloyd. 2016. "Breaking Boundaries of Role and Hierarchy in Collaborative Music-Making." *Contemporary Music Review* 35 (6): 630–47. DOI: 10.1080/07494467.2016.1282610

Attali, Jacques. 1985. *Noise: The Political Economy of Music*. Manchester: Manchester University Press.

Barron, Anne. 2006. "Copyright Law's Musical Work." *Social and Legal Studies* 15 (10): 101–26. DOI: 10.1177/0964663906060985

Beard, Alex. 2017. *Natural Born Learners*. London: Weidenfeld & Nicholson.

Becker, Howard S. 2008. *Art Worlds*. Berkeley CA & London: University of California Press.

Bennett, Joe. 2012. "Constraint, Collaboration and Creativity in Popular Songwriting Teams." In *The Act of Musical Composition*, edited by Dave Collins, 139–69. Farnham and Burlington VT: Ashgate.

Bowen, José A. 1993. "The History of Remembered Innovation: Tradition and Its Role in the Relationship between Musical Works and Their Performances." *The Journal of Musicology* 11 (2): 139–73. DOI: 10.1525/jm.1993.11.2.03a00010

Butt, John. 2018. "Monteverdi, the 1610 Vespers and the Beginnings of the Modern Musical Work." *Journal of the Royal Musical Association* 143 (1): 21–50. DOI: 10.1080/02690403.2018.1434328

Carroll, Noël. 2003. "Art, Creativity, and Tradition." In *The Creation of Art: New Essays in Philosophical Aesthetics*, edited by Berys Gaut & Paisley Livingstone, 208–34. Cambridge & New York: Cambridge University Press.

Casey, Rob. 2016. "Cage and Tudor as Process." *Contemporary Music Review* 35 (6): 670–85. DOI: 10.1080/07494467.2016.1282648

Clarke, Eric F. & Mark Doffman. 2017. *Distributed Creativity: Collaboration and Improvisation in Contemporary Music*. Oxford: Oxford University Press. DOI: 10.1093/oso/9780199355914.001.0001

Cook, Nicholas. 2001. "Between Process and Product." *Music Theory Online* 7 (2). Accessed 4 May 2015. www.mtosmt.org/issues/mto.01.7.2/mto.01.7.2.cook_frames.html

———. 2013. *Beyond the Score: Music as Performance*. Oxford and New York: Oxford University Press. DOI: 10.1093/acprof:oso/9780199357406.001.0001

———. 2018. *Music as Creative Practice*. Oxford: Oxford University Press. DOI: 10.1093/oso/9780199347803.001.0001

Crimp, Martin & George Benjamin. 2014. *Composition as Textual Illumination: Martin Crimp and George Benjamin Discuss Written on Skin*. Accessed 3 June 2017. www.contemporarytheatrereview.org/2014/video-written-on-skin/

Fitch, Fabrice & Neil Heyde. 2007. "'Recercar' – The Collaborative Process and Invention." *Twentieth-Century Music* 4 (1): 71–95. DOI: 10.1017/S1478572207000539

Glazner, Nancy. 2001. "Dialogic Subversion: Bakhtin, the Novel and Gertrude Stein." In *Bakhtin and Cultural Theory*, edited by Ken Shepherd & David Hirschkop, 155–76. Manchester: Manchester University Press.

Goehr, Lydia. 1992. *The Imaginary Museum of Musical Works: An Essay in the Philosophy of Music*. Oxford and New York: Oxford University Press. DOI: 10.1093/0198235410.001.0001

———. 1993. "'Music has No Meaning to Speak Of': On the Politics of Musical Interpretation." In *The Interpretation of Music: Philosophical Essays*, edited by Jennifer Judkins & Michael Krausz, 177–202. Oxford & New York: Oxford University Press.

Gorton, David & Stefan Östersjö. 2016. "Choose Your Own Adventure Music: On the Emergence of Voice in Musical Collaboration." *Contemporary Music Review* 35 (6): 579–98. DOI: 10.1080/07494467.2016.1282596

Guyer, Paul. 2003. "Exemplary Originality: Genius, Universality, and Individuality." In *The Creation of Art*, edited by Berys Gaut & Paisley Livingstone, 116–37. Cambridge and New York: Cambridge University Press.

Hankinson, Ann & Deborah O'Grady. 1981. "In Re: Collaboration." *Perspectives of New Music* 19 (1/2): 200–11. DOI: 10.2307/832591

Harley, James. 2008. "The Making of New Music: Composer as Collaborator." In *Compositional Crossroads: Music, McGill, Montreal*, by Eleanor Stubley, 129–49. Montreal and London: McGill-Queen's University Press.

Harrison, Ian. 2012. "An Exploration into the Uses of Extended Techniques in Works for the Saxophone, and How their Application may be Informed by a Contextual Understanding of the Works Themselves." Unpublished PhD thesis, University of Huddersfield.

Hastings, Baird. 1983. *Choreographer and Composer*. Boston MA: Twayne Publishers.

Hayden, Sam & Luke Windsor. 2007. "Collaboration and the Composer: Case Studies from the End of the 20th Century." *Tempo* 61 (2): 28–39. DOI: 10.1017/S0040298207000113

Johnson, Dr Samuel. 2016. *Samuel Johnson Soundbite*. Accessed 18 December 2018. samueljohnson.com/refuge.html.

John-Steiner, Vera. 2000. *Creative Collaboration*. Oxford: Oxford University Press. DOI: 10.1093/acprof:oso/9780195307702.001.0001

Jordan, Stephanie. 2000. *Dialogues with Music in Twentieth-Century Ballet*. London: Dance Books.

Kanga, Zubin R. 2014. "Inside the Collaborative Process: Realising New Works for Piano." Unpublished PhD Thesis, Royal Academy of Music, London.

Konečni, Vladimir J. 2012. "'Composers' Creative Process: the Role of Life-Events, Emotion and Reason." In *Musical Imaginations: Multidisciplinary Perspectives on Creativity, Performance, and Perception*, edited by David J. Hargreaves, Dorothy E. Miell & Raymond A.R. MacDonald, 141–55. Oxford: Oxford University Press. DOI: 10.1093/acprof:oso/9780199568086.001.0001

Kounios, John & Mark Beeman. 2015. *The Eureka Factor: Creative Insights and the Brain*. London: Windmill Books.

Leech-Wilkinson, Daniel. 2012. "Compositions, Scores, Performances, Meanings." *Music Theory Online* 1 (18). Accessed 7 June 2018. mtosmt.org/issues/mto.12.18.1/mto.12.18.1.leech-wilkinson.php

Lindon, Adam & Eric F. Clarke. 2017. "Distributed Cognition, Ecological Theory and Groups Improvisation." In *Distributed Creativity: Collaboration and Improvisation in Contemporary Music*, edited by Eric F. Clarke & Mark Doffman, 52–69. Oxford: Oxford University Press. DOI: 10.1093/oso/9780199355914.001.0001

Lucas, Caroline. 2016. "Multiple Radical Forms Comma Traces Creativity of Constraint: A Piece for Solo Voice and Various Accompaniment." In *Gender, Age, and Musical Creativity*, edited by Catherine Haworth & Lisa Colton, 185–201. Abingdon and New York: Routledge.

McClary, Susan. 1987. "The Blasphemy of Talking Politics During Bach Year." In *Music and Society*, edited by Richard Leppert & Susan McClary, 13–62. Cambridge and New York: Cambridge University Press.

Novitz, David. 2003. "Explanations of Creativity." In *The Creation of Art: New Essays in Philosophical Aesthetics*, edited by Berys Gaut & Paisley Livingstone, 174–91. Cambridge & New York: Cambridge University Press.

Östersjö, Stefan. 2008. *SHUT UP 'N' PLAY! Negotiating the Musical Work.* Unpublished PhD thesis, Lund: Lund University.
Picasso, Pablo. 2016. "Pablo Picasso Quotes." *BrainyQuote.* Accessed 19 July 2018. www.brainyquote.com/quotes/pablo_picasso_104106
Redhead, Lauren. 2016. "'New Music' as Patriarchal Category." In *Gender, Age, and Musical Creativity*, edited by Catherine Haworth & Lisa Colton, 171–84. Abingdon and New York: Routledge.
Roche, Heather. 2011. "Dialogue and Collaboration in the Creation of New Works for Clarinet." Unpublished PhD thesis, University of Huddersfield.
Roe, Paul. 2007. "A Phenomenology of Collaboration in Collaboration in Contemporary Composition and Performance." Unpublished PhD Thesis, University of York.
Sawyer, Keith & Stacy DeZutter. 2009. "Distributed Creativity: How Collective Creations Emerge from Collaboration." *Psychology of Aesthetics, Creativity, and the Arts* 3 (2): 81–92. psycnet.apa.org/record/2009-06908-008
Sawyer, Keith. 2006. *Explaining Creativity: The Science of Human Innovation.* Oxford & New York: Oxford University Press.
———. 2014. "Musical Performance as Collaborative Practice." In *Collaborative Creative Thought and Practice in Music*, edited by Margaret S. Barrett, 271–86. Abingdon and New York: Ashgate Publishing. DOI: 10.4324/9781315572635
Schoenberg, Arnold. 1975. *Style and Idea: Selected Writings of Arnold Schoenberg.* Edited by Leonard Stein. Translated by Leo Black. Berkley CA: University of California Press.
Schwarz, Boris. 1983. "Joseph Joachim and the Genesis of Brahms's Violin Concerto." *The Musical Quarterly* 69 (4): 503–26. DOI: 10.1093/mq/LXIX.4.503
Sloman, Steven & Philip Fernbach. 2011. *The Knowledge Illusion: Why We Never Think Alone.* New York: Farrar, Strauss, and Giroux.
Small, Christopher. 1998. *Musicking: The Meanings of Performing and Listening.* Middletown CT: Wesleyan University Press.
Stiefel, Van. 2006. *A Study of Choreographer/Composer Collaboration.* Accessed 6 May 2019. www.researchgate.net/publication/24116919_A_Study_of_the_ChoreographerComposer_Collaboration
Styles, Luke. 2016. "Handspun, the Role of Collaboration and Embodiment as Compositional Process: a Transdisciplinary Perspective." *Contemporary Music Review* 35 (6): 612–29. DOI: 10.1080/07494467.2016.1282598
Till, Nicholas. 1992. *Mozart and the Enlightenment: Truth, Virtue and Beauty in Mozart's Operas.* London: Faber and Faber Ltd.
Toynbee, Jason. 2017. "The Labour that Dare not Speak Its Name: Musical Creativity, Labour Process and the Materials of Music." In *Distributed Creativity: Collaboration and Improvisation in Contemporary Music*, edited by Eric F. Clarke & Mark Doffman, 37–51. Oxford: Oxford University Press. DOI: 10.1093/oso/9780199355914.001.0001
Trillo, Roberto Alonso. 2019. *Death and (Re)Birth of J. S. Bach: Reconsidering Musical Authorship and the Work-Concept.* Abingdon and New York: Routledge. DOI: 10.4324/9780429504716

Watts, Carol. 2010. "Set, Unset: Collaboration, Encounter and the Scene of Poetry." *Contemporary Music Review* 29 (2): 145–58. DOI: 10.1080/07494467.2010.534921

White, Harry. 1997. "'If It's Baroque, Don't Fix It': Reflections on Lydia Goehr's 'Work-Concept' and the Historical Integrity of Musical Composition." *Acta Musicologica* 59: 94–104. DOI: 10.2307/932803

Wiggins, Geraint A. 2012. "The Mind's Chorus: Creativity Before Consciousness." *Cognitive Computing* 4: 306–19. DOI: 10.1007/s12559-012-9151-6

2 The musical imagination as dialogue

Introduction

Musical imagination cannot be an ability limited to a few gifted people, since we all apply our imaginations in responding to musical experiences and trying to make sense of them. As I noted in the Introduction, this universal ability is applied in essentially the same way whether inventing musical ideas to notate, playing music from notation, inventing while improvising, or when listening.

The evidence suggests that the imaginative process has three main characteristics:

1. Ideas and understandings emerge from interactions between the many influences a person has absorbed, and so are inherently complex and 'ambiguous'.
2. The imagination depends on, and is provoked by, engagement with society and the wider environment.
3. Ideas appear in the conscious mind as if from nowhere following subconscious rumination.

By 'ambiguous' I don't intend the meaning commonly implied today of 'confusing', but that musical ideas can be interpreted in more than one way simultaneously. That is what William Empson meant by the word in his classic study of literature, *Seven Types of Ambiguity*, in which he analysed ways in which poets embed complexity of meaning in their work (Empson 1930). To me, ambiguity in this sense is a characteristic of all art and distinguishes it from the more narrowly functional.

The imaginative process has been described in ways close to that outlined above by writers who approach the subject from different perspectives. For instance, Deleuze and Guattari, who, as a philosopher and a psychoanalyst, collaborated on writings central to the development of post-structuralist thinking, describe how:

> To write is perhaps to bring this assemblage of the unconscious to the light of day, to select the whispering voices, to gather the tribes and secret idioms from which I extract something I call my Self.
>
> (2016, 98)

This is close to the ethnomusicologist John Blacking's view that 'Each apparently new idea in music ... grows out of a composer's experience of his environment ...' (1971, 72–3) and to literary analysts Wimsatt and Beardsley's view that 'There is a gross body of life, of sensory and mental experience, which lies behind and in some sense causes every poem ...' (1954, 12). Each of these writers refers to a multitude of stimuli provoking the imagination, and to ideas somehow emerging from this intermingling of influences. It seems significant to me that such similar views of the imagination are described by writers from contrasting backgrounds. My aim here is to define this view in more detail and to show that it is supported by modern evidence of how our thinking processes work.

I've divided this chapter into two parts. In Part 1 I suggest a view of how the musical imagination works. In Part 2 I examine descriptions by composers and other artists of the working of their imaginations to see whether these correspond with the view suggested in the first part.

Part 1: Theory

Complexity and dialogue

We all recognise that we encounter many things which influence us. It is also our experience that ideas appear in our heads as if from nowhere, though on reflection they can sometimes be traced back to specific influences. My concern here is with the process between absorbing influences and having ideas, a process which I argue consists of a subconscious dialogue and a dialogue through which the influences absorbed are multiplied and changed. The fruits of this dialogue are the ideas which pop into our minds, and since these emerge from the intermingling of many influences they have complexity or ambiguity embedded within them. The key point here is that there is an internal process which we cannot fully explain to ourselves – an inner voice – and my argument is that this arises from a dialogue between influences.

This idea can be traced back at least as far as Plato's account of Socrates' speech in his defence at his trial, known as the *Apology*. Socrates refers to being driven by an inner voice which led him to teach in ways considered unacceptable by his accusers. In one translation, Socrates describes this as '… an oracle or sign which comes to me … a kind of voice.' (Plato 2016, 25). In this description, the voice had two characteristics: it came from within, and he was unable to explain it. My argument is that this inner voice springs from a dialogue between the many influences we have absorbed and that its resulting complexity is the one the voice cannot be readily explained.

The same concept is found in the Judeo-Christian tradition in the form of the '… still small voice' (Bible 1957, I Kings 19:12, 292) through which God is said to have spoken to Elijah and which is sometimes interpreted as the voice of conscience. The nature of this voice is that it is heard, and we somehow know what we must do even though we may not be able to explain this to ourselves.

The other concept central to the idea of the inner dialogue is the view of psychologist William James that personality is multiple rather than singular, with each person not a simple self but the focus of a complex of inter-relationships (James 1890, 291). This view leads directly to the idea of the complex intermingling of influences from which ideas emerge. The use of the term 'dialogue' for this internal process grew from Mikhail Bakhtin's (1981) analysis of novels as a dialogic form of art. The inner voice through which ideas come to us is seen as the outcome of a dialogue between elements within our multi-faceted individuality.

These three ideas of the inner voice, the self as a multitude of interactions and experiences, and dialogue, have been brought together by modern psychologists such as Hermans and Kempen (1993) in the concept of the dialogic self. They argue that human behaviour is based on interaction and dialogue beginning with the mother–infant relationship, and describe a person's identity not as something separate from other people but as dialogic, writing that:

> Since the *Me* is also a 'social *Me*,' they [people] are not able to think, feel, or act in isolation from the community in which they participate. They are continuously involved in dialogues …
> (1993, 72)

I will quote numerous writers in support of the concept of the inner dialogue as the source of ideas. First, though, it is important to examine how the idea of the dialogic imagination developed from the writing of Bakhtin on the novel. After all, he introduced the term 'dialogic' to characterise an <u>effect</u> rather than a cause, since he used it to describe the multi-referential character of novels resulting from the interaction of the characters, their modes of speech and behaviour, and the worlds of experience which each brings to the novel. His other key term, 'heteroglossia' (1981, 263), refers to the wide range of connections and connotations which enter a novel with the contrasting characters, each with their different backgrounds, memories, and experiences. These combine to form the varied (hetero) set of connotations and references (glossary) which gives novels their rich character.

However, Bakhtin's term 'dialogic' has been widely used for the <u>cause</u> of the complexity of novels, on the grounds that the imagination must be stimulated by a dialogue between many influences to be able to produce dialogic art such as novels. For this reason, the term has been widely used to describe the way the imagination operates, for example by Fernyhough (2016), Fontaine and Hunter (2006), Glazner (2001), and Shepherd (2001).

The way Bakhtin's thinking developed during his life provides justification for this usage. He first put forward his '… revolutionary concept of "dialogism" …' (Holquist 1981, xxiv) in a book on Dostoevsky published in 1929, arguing that novels are founded on verbal interaction or dialogue between characters (1981, 259). He initially saw poetry differently from novels, and argued that 'The language of the poet [unlike that of the novelist] is *his* language, he is utterly immersed in it … as pure and direct expression of his own intention.' (1981, 285). Since Bakhtin did not see the poet's language as dialogic, but different from that reflected in the novel, it follows that the novelist's imagination, as well as their novels, must be rooted in dialogue. Dialogic art can only result from a dialogic imagination.

Modern writers have extended the use of the term dialogic to all the arts and to the human imaginative process in general. As Donin explains, the dialogic process in musical composition concerns '… a 'dialogical self' in whose imagination the influence of forerunners, as well as fellow composers, performers and audiences, play a part in the creative process.' (2017, 85). It is this dialogue between influences which leads to the sudden appearance of ideas in the mind, and to the emergence of ideas in which complexity and ambiguity are embedded.

So far so good, but an understanding is needed of the operation of the dialogic imagination to complete the picture since the evidence is that much of the process is subconscious. I'll come back to this later; but first, it is important to look at how we absorb the stimuli which mingle in our internal dialogues since the way in which this takes place is central how the dialogic imagination works.

Environmental engagement and imaginative learning

Learning and imagining are connected with our social and wider environments, and our mental processes are not separable from our engagement with the world around us. The consequence is that the dialogues from which our ideas and understandings arise are provoked by our active involvement with, and response to, our environment.

We are, however, selective in the way we engage in our environment, and how we are influenced by social contact and the non-human. After all, we engage in with some stimuli and contacts but not others, or some more than others, so the process is clearly not a passive one of absorbing influences. Rather, the evidence is that we have ideas due to our active direct or indirect engagement with people and the non-human world around us. This view helps to bridge a gap which has been identified in our understanding of the imagination.

I referred earlier to a collection of essays on the musical imagination edited by Hargreaves, Miell, and MacDonald (2012). In the concluding chapter, Cook reviews the wide-ranging contributions to the book and draws the conclusion that there is an '... irresolvable tension ...' (2012, 455) between studies of the way music-making is influenced by external influences (sociocultural and ecological studies) and studies of the mental processes which operate when imagining. On the one hand, several studies in the book show how imaginative work is affected by external influences. On the other hand, the book includes studies of the mental processes which operate as we imagine. Cook's view is that there is tension between findings in these two areas of study and that this is irresolvable. His view appears to be based on the difficulty of demonstrating a connection between external influences and internal processes. The findings of the studies I refer to in this section and the next go some way towards resolving this tension.

This brings me to the second figure from the early years of the Soviet Union, after Bakhtin, whose research is relevant to this subject, Lev Vygotsky. Like Bakhtin's, his research has come back into prominence in recent years. His studies concerned mainly the process of learning and specifically learning by children. He found that children learned principally through interaction with others, rather than being passive recipients of knowledge taught to them. He concluded that '... human learning presupposes a specific social nature and a process by which children grow into the intellectual life of those around them.' (1978,

88). He described how children develop through experiences and their reactions to them, unlike plants passing through pre-determined stages of growth (1978, 20). He concluded that:

> The path from object to child and from child to object passes through another person. This complex human structure is the product of a developmental process deeply rooted in the links between individual and social history.
>
> (1978, 30)

While his findings relate to learning, they apply equally to the imagination since his finding was that learning is an imaginative process. This link between his conclusions and the nature of the imagination has been made by modern writers such as Guimaraes Lima (1995, 412), and Mahn and John-Steiner (2002). The latter consider that Vygotsky saw thought as arising from affect and emotion rather than from other thoughts (2002, 47). We create knowledge in response to the feelings which result from our experiences of direct or indirect interaction with other people and our environment, rather than from of being taught or learning information.

The same conclusion is drawn by Small, who notes the shift away from the legacy of Descartes' thinking, in which 'Knowledge exists "out there," independently of who knows it, pre-existing any possible knower of it, and continuing after any knower has ceased to exist.' (1998, 50). He considers that modern studies in philosophy and neurology had shown that '... image formation is an active and creative process, not mere passive reception of whatever stimuli are being presented.' (1998, 54). As Reybrouck puts it, '... knowledge must be constructed through interaction with the environment ...' (2006, 51), tracing this idea back to Piaget (1967) and Dewey (1933). We make our own knowledge as imaginative participants in the learning process.

Approaching the same question from a different direction, Beard notes that children learn to speak through being spoken to rather than by overhearing speech (2017, 61). He quotes a study led by Kuhl (2003) of attempts to teach Chinese to Western children by various methods. The only children who learned anything were those spoken to in Chinese. In a related study it was found that, if parents made eye contact as their infant babbled, the child was likely to use more words as a toddler (Donnellan, et al. 2019, 1). These studies show that the interaction with the other person is fundamental to the learning process. Beard describes how as 'Infant humans [we] didn't only regurgitate; we created, made new meanings, shared feelings.' (Beard 2017, 63).

A study of human perception and development by Damasio (2018) lends support to the view that learning takes place in response to senses and feelings, and so through interaction. He shows that humans sense our environment, as do any other creatures, and these senses provoke feelings which then lead us to imagine understandings. His argument is that senses and the resulting emotions are the way in which organisms perceive the world. Humans' high level of ability is, then, the result not of superior analytical intelligence but of thinking provoked by a superior ability to sense, experience, and imagine. The same argument, that our process of perception is emotion-guided and imaginative, is put forward by Noordhof, who writes that '... our experience of expressive properties ... essentially involves *the sensuous imagination (through simulation) of an emotion-guided process ...*' (2008, 337).

This view that we learn actively from experiences and social contact, and that learning results from the ability to experience and feel, has the important implication that the learning and imaginative processes are the same. We use our imaginations to create our knowledge just as when imagining ideas. Both learning and imagining result from the stimulus of active engagement with other people and our environment, and so they are intrinsically connected to, and result from, engagement with the world around us.

This same conclusion is drawn by neuroscientist Buzsáki (2019) from his studies of the way the brain forms information, that is, how we learn. In his view, theories of the brain have wrongly relied mainly on computer-based metaphors in which the brain is seen as receiving information from outside in the form of stimuli and being formed by these. These metaphors are based on the presumption that the brain starts as a blank slate like an un-programmed computer and is then programmed by the stimuli which it receives. Knowledge is therefore seen as the result of the absorption of external stimuli. Buzsáki points out that the weakness of these models is that they presume some unexplained method by which the brain selects which inputs to absorb, since it does not attend to external stimuli equally but selects some and ignores others.

He proposes instead that as soon as an infant is born it is evident that their brain is working on the basis of structures and quasi-understandings which are already there. In his view, this is how humans continue to perceive during life, through the construction of understandings of new experiences on the basis of existing perceptions, rather than just by absorbing information presented to us. Damasio reached the same conclusion earlier, writing that 'At birth, the human brain comes to development endowed with drives and instincts ...' (2006, 126). The evidence, then, is that our imaginations actively construct ideas from our sensory responses to the people and the world around us. Rather than being taught knowledge by other people, we make our own understandings and ideas in response to social and environmental stimuli.

This active engagement is, of course, not only social but encompasses the non-human world around us. We respond to our social and non-human environments in similar ways, developing feelings in response to our inextricable entanglement in the non-human world as physical beings ourselves. However, it is disputed whether this engagement takes the same form as that with people.

On one level, this environmental engagement results from using physical means and objects, for instance, to make music. A composer writing notation on manuscript paper, perhaps testing ideas using a piano, or writing into notation software on a computer, is inextricably engaged with those non-human objects to the extent that their thinking and writing is inseparable from them, not merely affected by their nature. Interaction with musical instruments, whether imagining them to write or using them to perform, is another part of this inextricable link between the human and the non-human in the processes of imagining music. It is hard, or perhaps impossible, to think and imagine except in terms of the objects and technologies we use and depend on.

However, whether this takes the same form as our social engagement is disputed. This disagreement centres around Actor-Network Theory (ANT), the view that we are inextricable parts of networks of the human and non-human. The French philosopher Bruno Latour, in particular, argues that we do not live independently of such networks, and there can be no actor independent of a network or such a thing as an external observer (Latour 1996, 381). ANT involves '… abandoning any distinction between natural and social phenomenon.' (Crawford 2004). There is no need, for the purposes of this discussion, to go deeply into this question,[1] but it is worth noting a key point made in a review of the dispute between Latour and his critics. The reviewer, Kipnis, argues that living and non-living things should not be treated as undifferentiated actors in networks since living things actively seek to maintain themselves and have intentions, whereas non-living things have an effect on living things but do not have such intentions. He sees the idea of '… anthropomorphic ascriptions of agency as a fallacy.' (Kipnis 2015, 49). That is, things, and in terms of whether we take account of them that mostly includes non-human living things, do not have articulated intentions to which humans respond.

To get back to music, an oboist, a composer imagining an oboe when writing, or a listener hearing the sound and seeing the player with the instrument, will imagine within the possibilities of the oboe, and be constrained by its limitations. But the oboe has no intentions; it simply is as it is. The musical imagination, whilst deeply affected by the objects and technologies involved in music-making, appears to have different relationships with the social environment and the non-human world since with the former we find ourselves responding to people who have intentions distinct from our own.

To return to the key point in this discussion, there is an accumulation of evidence from Vygotsky's studies onwards showing that learning and imagining result from the feelings provoked by active responses to our experience of the social and non-human environment. This engagement stimulates us to make our own understandings and imagine ideas. The consequence, as Damasio argues, is that cultural artefacts emerge from '… interactions between individuals and environment …' (Damasio 2001, 59).

This is the first step in bridging the gap identified by Cook (2012) between studies of the external influences on music and those of the mental processes involved. The mental processes are not just influenced by the external environment as if they were passive but consist of actively making ideas in response to experiences. Of course, we remain a long way from demonstrating direct connections between brain activity and specific external influences, but it can be said that the internal processes consist of, and result from, active engagement with external influences.

Experience is the food of the imagination.

The subconscious dialogue

The third part of my argument, and my other contribution towards resolving the 'tension' between the findings of environmental and psychological studies of the musical imagination, is that this socially-activated dialogue is largely subconscious. A musician or audience member actively absorbs a multitude of influences. These, so to speak, disappear into the subconscious where they multiply through dialogue. Musical ideas or understandings may then appear, arising from the influences we have absorbed and the dialogues between them, and popping into the conscious mind as if from nowhere. Descriptions of musical composition, as Wiggins comments, often show that '… an idea appears in consciousness without warning, and without any indication of whence it came.' (2012, 306). The title of Wiggins' paper is

The Mind's Chorus, and he argues that there is a constant churning of our subconscious thoughts from which ideas occasionally appear in our conscious minds. He describes the:

> non-conscious creativity [that] is happening all the time as a result of ongoing anticipation in all sensory (and other) modalities. When conditions are right, this ... gives rise to creativity as a side effect.
>
> (2012, 315)

A description of this process of subconscious churning of influences and possibilities, or dialogue, is found in an account by the mathematician Henri Poincaré. He is quoted by Ghiselin as explaining how ideas would appear as if from nowhere, but also that the disorder from which they emerged was an essential part of the imaginative process. He described how:

> Ideas rose in crowds; I felt them collide until pairs interlocked, so to speak, making a stable combination. Only certain ones are harmonious, and, consequently, are at once useful and beautiful ... Only this disorder itself permits unexpected combination.
>
> (1952, 36)

This view of the subconscious dialogue is supported by the research of psychologist Charles Fernyhough (2016), who shows in his book *The Voices Within* that people think in a form of dialogic inner speech. He notes how young children discuss with themselves what they are doing as they play, and that this dialogic way of thinking becomes internalised and subconscious as we grow up. He describes his studies of people at the moments when they are listening to their inner voice and shows that this voice is dialogic; that is, it consists of a person having a dialogue with themselves. He proposes a:

> Dialogic Thinking model [in which] ... there is a group of mental functions – operations that our minds can perform – which depend on an interplay between different perspectives on reality. They involve taking a point of view, and then taking another one, and enacting a dialogue between them.
>
> (2016, 99)

Referring to the voices in our heads and the dialogues between them, he writes that '... the mysteries of inner speech become more comprehensible when we recognise that it has the properties of a dialogue.' (2016, 15). The view that ideas originate in the subconscious is supported by the findings of the studies by Kounios and Beeman (2015) and Konečni (2012), quoted in Chapter 1, showing that when a person has an idea, parts of the brain linked to subconscious thought are activated prior to those linked to conscious thought. In other words, ideas can be tracked developing in the subconscious mind before we become aware of them. While these neurological findings concern the development of an idea in the subconscious immediately prior to its appearance in the conscious mind, the examples quoted below on the effect of taking a break suggest that a longer subconscious process of rumination must operate before ideas form in this way.

Further evidence in support of the existence of subconscious thinking is provided by recent research on whether it would be possible to train people in the use of their subconscious mental capacities. A team led by Cortese (2020) carried out carefully controlled experiments in which participants were rewarded if they gave correct answers, even though choosing these answers depended on mental activity of which they were not aware. They report that their experiments were successful (2020, 8) and so show not only that subconscious thought exists but also that our subconscious thinking can be enhanced through practice.

The same subconscious process appears to be at work in the musical imagination, as Bailes and Bishop show in their review of the relevant research. They write, concerning musical composition, that 'While inspiration may strike as a seemingly complete idea, it is likely to be based on the unconscious amalgamation of assimilated musical experience.' (2012, 60). This description could be broadened to include the influence of any experience absorbed into the musician's subconscious mind.

The view that ideas emerge from subconscious thinking is challenged by Perkins, who argues that '… extended unconscious thinking probably does not occur.' (1981, 52) and queries the accuracy of another account by Henri Poincaré. The latter described how the solution to a mathematical problem suddenly occurred to him on stepping onto a train without having been aware of thinking about it in the preceding period. Perkins disputes Poincaré's account and argues that '… he didn't tell it rightly. I have never heard of a completely out-of-the-blue insight when a person had reviewed the thinking immediately afterwards.' (1981, 49). Perkins reports that experiments on the existence of a non-conscious incubation process have proved negative, and queries descriptions such as Poincaré's, arguing that accounts of recalled experience are often unreliable. However, there are several grounds for rejecting Perkins' conclusion. These are that:

- More recent work by psychologists and neurologists such as Wiggins, Fernyhough, Konečni, and Kounios and Beeman demonstrates that ideas do in fact develop in the subconscious prior to a person becoming conscious of them.
- Perkins refers to ideas coming '… completely out-of-the-blue.' (1981, 52). This seems to me to be a misnomer, though he may not have meant to imply that thoughts in fact arise from nothing. The evidence from accounts of the emergence of ideas from subconscious rumination is that the person had previously been aware of the subject or problem. They stopped thinking about it, and an idea or solution later appeared in their mind. In Poincaré's case, for instance, the solution which suddenly occurred to him was to a problem with which he was familiar, but he had not been aware of thinking about it.
- Accounts of ideas appearing as if from nowhere are simply too numerous to dismiss in this way, and I will quote many in Part 2. They cannot all have failed to 'tell it rightly'.

The view that subconscious rumination takes place prior to the emergence of ideas is evidenced by the many descriptions of their arrival when distracted by walking, travelling, or after taking a break. Ideas seem to emerge from the subconscious when the conscious mind is otherwise occupied in these ways. Kounios and Beeman quote the example of Herman von Helmholtz, an eminent late-nineteenth-century scientist, who described how solutions to problems he had been working on '… liked especially to make their appearance while I was taking an easy walk over wooded hills in sunny weather.' (2015, 29). Bailes and Bishop note similar experiences, including composers who developed ideas on bicycle rides, those who went for a walk when blocked, and the well-known example of Mozart developing ideas when travelling by carriage or walking (2012, 70).

Accounts of Beethoven, Mahler, and Britten examined by Predota (2019) show that they liked to take walks, notebook in pocket, since they found that musical ideas would occur to them when distracted in this way. Gluck was said to write best when sitting in a field, and Mozart found that ideas came to him when playing billiards. Britten, Rossini, and Richard Strauss each noted how they found that ideas occurred to them while taking a break (Predota 2019). Bailes and Bishop quote Stockhausen recalling '… that very often when I'd worked until late at night, I gave up; the brain continued working on the problem during my sleep, and I knew the solution next morning.' (2012, 61).

These composers evidently found the distraction of walking, observing things around them, playing a game, or simply taking a break or sleeping, allowed their subconscious mind to incubate ideas. This same pattern was found in several of the studies reviewed by Konečni, who notes that 'Once an impasse is reached, relaxation and letting the mind wander are helpful ...' (2012, 143–4). The subconscious dialogue is then freer to do its work.

One feature of the dialogic imagination is therefore that ideas appear as if from nowhere, at times which cannot be predicted, and often after distraction rather than from concentrated thought. Another is that an idea can somehow feel 'right', a sense often described as a 'gut' feeling or the equivalent of the 'still, small voice' telling a person that something is right or wrong. As an example, McCutchan quotes one of the composers she interviewed as saying 'Where did all this music come from? I don't remember! You might have six or eight ideas, and one of them seems like the right thing to work on.' (1999, 183). In other words, they had the ability to select between many alternatives without being conscious of how they did so.

There is a risk of describing this process as if it were purely a matter of brain activity, and my reference to gut feeling in the last paragraph was a deliberate corrective to this. The question of why artists have a subconscious sense that an idea is 'right' or 'wrong' brings me to the subject of embodied perception or cognition, which forms an important part of the discussion in Chapter 4 on how listeners make sense of music. The view that cognition is embodied could help explain why the subconscious dialogue results not only in ideas, but a sense of whether those ideas are right or not in the context concerned.

A possible explanation for this process is suggested by Damasio in his earlier book, *Descartes' Error* (2006), in which he argues that Descartes was wrong in taking the view that '... the soul by which I am what I am, is entirely distinct from the body.' (Descartes 1970, 101), that is, thinking and feeling take place in the mind, which is separate from the body. Damasio shows, quoting numerous examples including patients of his as a neurologist, how bodily and 'mental' sensing and thinking are one integrated process. Many of his examples are of people who had damage to the parts of the brain which integrate signals from the body with those from other brain regions. This damage often leaves them unable to judge the appropriateness of their actions or to make choices between alternatives. One of the patients Damasio describes at length (2006, Ch. 3) showed two main symptoms, a lack of emotion and the inability to make choices. Damasio makes a connection between these and explains the difficulty in making choices in terms of the inability to 'feel' what was right. It is this ability, rooted in an integrated body/brain process, which is likely to underlie the process by which potentially valuable ideas emerge from the disorder described by Poincaré (Ghiselin 1952, 36) and also the way in which we come to feel they are 'right' in the context concerned.

From this, Damasio argues that our integrated bodily systems and senses are fundamental to our ability to make choices, writing that '... a biological mechanism makes the preselection, examines candidates, and allows only a few to present themselves ...' (2006, 189). That is, this integrated body/brain process enables us to narrow down choices so that only those which 'feel right' appear in the conscious mind. This finding could explain both why ideas appear after subconscious rumination and the subconscious sense that an idea is 'right' in the context concerned. Damasio's argument is that our integrated process of sensing enables us to reflect on ideas and alternatives, to generate new potential solutions, and to choose between them, without our being fully aware of how we are doing so. Ideas, or potential solutions to problems, then appear in the conscious mind as if from nowhere, and are felt to be 'right', or subsequently rejected as 'wrong' following further embodied subconscious reflection.

The suggestion, then, is that the imagination is embodied, with ideas appearing in our conscious minds due to a wider process of bodily sensing rather than just brain activity. The term 'embodied music cognition' (Leman 2008) is used in music for this integrated process involving our entire physical selves. While cause and effect between neurological activity and thinking processes remains hard to demonstrate, the evidence does suggest that the process of imaginative rumination may be experienced as subconscious because it relies on an integrated body/brain process. Further research on this could prove valuable.

The idea of the embodied subconscious is close to the process described by Godøy as an '... incessant simulation of various body movements ...' (2010, 108) as we engage with things we either see or only assume. He shows how bodies shape the way music emerges, and how listeners covertly or overtly simulate the bodily motions involved in producing the music they are hearing, imitating the sound-producing motions (Godøy 2018, 2.5). Writing with a team of researchers, he describes how they found performance to be '... *a transformation of the score to a series of coarticulated human motion chunks and sonic objects.*' and not only a subjective interpretation of the music (2005, 6.3). They also show that forms of 'air playing' are frequently observed among listeners. In related research, Haueisen and

Knösche found that involuntary finger movements are often triggered in pianists when listening to piano music (2001).

The view that we engage bodily as we imagine or re-imagine music is now well established, and connects with Damasio's (2006) argument that the appearance of ideas and the sense of their 'rightness' results from the integration of our brains and wider bodily sensing. This may offer an explanation for the experience that the imagination resides in the subconscious. Ideas appear to emerge as if from nowhere, and the sense that they are right or wrong in the context emerges in the same way.

Implications of this view

My suggested view of the musical imagination is, therefore, that ideas and understandings arise in the individual mind from an environmentally activated and embodied subconscious dialogue. This view complements the idea of distributed creativity, that music results from the creative contributions of many people. Together they offer an alternative to the stereotype of the 'genius' as the source of imagination in music, inventing from their own mind alone.

In that sense, however, there does remain a mysterious element to the musical imagination in that composers, performers, and listeners may not be conscious of, or understand, the operation of their imaginations. In fact, if the view I have put forward is correct, it must be impossible for anyone to fully understand their imaginative process since much of it is subconscious. While there is a risk that this lack of understanding may feed a musician's sense that they imagine just from within their own mind, there is no justification for this. A person may not fully understand how their own imagination works, but that doesn't mean that the imaginative process cannot be understood.

This conclusion has implications for the aspects of the musical imagination which I will examine in the next two chapters. The first concerns the consequence of subconscious thinking. If this is the way musicians imagine, with a far-from-complete awareness of their own imaginative process, then they may only be able to explain in a partial way what it is they are imagining. This is bound to constrain their ability to communicate with their partners when working on collaborative projects. That is the subject of Chapter 3.

The second implication follows from the view that the subconscious process through which musical ideas arise is affected by many influences which multiply through dialogue. Music, as a result, has complexity and ambiguity embedded within it and so will always be open to a variety of understandings and interpretations. This calls into question the idea of music as the communication of meanings by artists to audiences; an idea reflected in attempts to define the meaning of pieces of music. I deal with this question in Chapter 4, where I suggest an alternative explanation for why and how listeners experience music as meaningful.

Part 2: Accounts by composers (and others)

So much for theory. There are a good few accounts by composers and other artists of how they imagine, and several studies of their imaginative processes. The question is whether these examples correspond with my suggestion on how the imagination works.

It is important to remember, however, that accumulating descriptions of imagining in music or other art cannot prove my suggestions on how the musical imagination works to be correct, only that they are credible.

It is also important to be aware of the potential unreliability of accounts of recalled experience. Nisbett and Wilson (1977), for instance, argue that there is a tendency to rationalise accounts of experience in terms of plausible explanations, and a risk that people may report what they think should have taken place. Perkins adds that accounts can be distorted because people suffer from '... problems of memory loss, bias, [and the] unwarranted filling in of gaps in plausible ways ...' (1981, 26), but notes that asking people to record their thoughts immediately after they have had them is likely to result in more accurate reporting (1981, 32).

Other writers rate the value of accounts of experience more highly. Ericsson and Simon (1984, 371–3), for example, consider that the richness of verbal reports can be a valuable contribution to the study of cognitive processes as long as they are combined with other data.

That is my approach. I suggested that the imaginative process has three key characteristics and based that view on theoretical argument and extensive research findings. To compare that view with reports by artists of their imaginative processes is a valid way of combining rich descriptions with solid evidence. Certainly, on the key point that artists often say they do not know where their ideas come from, it is hard to see how they could be rationalising their accounts, as Sloboda (1999, 121–2) points out.

Descriptions and studies of the subject suggest that there are two features of the musical imagination and that the imaginative process is applied to two distinct activities, so I've grouped the accounts under these headings.

Two features of the imagination

Composers have often reported that the imaginative process begins with an initial idea popping into their mind. For instance, Beethoven, replying to one of his correspondents, wrote 'You may ask me where I obtain my ideas. I cannot answer this with any clarity. They come unbidden ...' (Hamburger 1992, 485). Tchaikovsky had the same experience, describing how 'The germ of a future composition comes suddenly and unexpectedly....' (2004, 274). A key aspect of their descriptions is that they experienced the process in a passive way. Ideas appeared in their minds apparently as if of their own accord.

A similar account, of the imaginative process of composer Phillippe Leroux, is given by Donin and Thereau, who describe how he would '... let a musical impression that could be potentially productive to his compositional work just "come to him", and note its essential features as rapidly as possible.' (2007, 236). Again, the process was experienced as passive.

In another study, Donin and Féron examine the working processes of a composer on one of his pieces. They describe how '*Gramiga*'s [the piece] beginning grew from limited material: a short musical cell for cimbalon, the idea of which came to the composer after a first fruitless attempt to begin composing.' (2012, 272). It seems that the composer was actively seeking musical ideas but, after he stopped, a suitable idea just occurred to them.

In an interview, John Taverner describes the invention of musical ideas as '... something that comes from deep inside one and takes one by surprise, quite honestly. I'm not aware of any conscious deliberation while I'm at work.' (1999, 132). He adds that 'All during this time the notes and patterns of notes are beginning to form in my head. I don't know where they come from.' (1999, 144). The composer Aaron Copland, reflecting the same sense of how his imagination works, writes that 'The composer is a kind of magician; out of the recesses of his thought he produces, or finds himself in possession of, the generative idea.' (1953, 42). Again, he found that ideas just appeared in his mind.

A study of twelve electro-acoustic composers by Delalande includes further examples of ideas popping suddenly into consciousness. The composers were asked to produce pieces for a research project, and he comments that 'The [initial] idea is not the result of the work being carried out but comes to mind or appears on its own in the course of an 'exploration'.' (2007, 18). He gives examples of composers who relied on chance discovery and then selected ideas which pleased them, who imagined the type of thing they were listening for in advance of hearing specific ideas, or who had a precise idea of the form of a planned piece but then relied on chance discovery for specific ideas. Some of the composers clearly had a better idea of what they were listening for than others, but they all then waited until material which pleased them appeared in their conscious minds.

In one of his books, *The Musical Mind*, Sloboda quotes descriptions of the imaginative process by Richard Strauss, Beethoven, Roger Sessions, and in a statement attributed to Mozart (1999, 115). In each case, the composer reported that they could not say where their ideas came from, or that ideas simply appeared in their mind. They all reported that thoughts on their pieces came to them as musical ideas. Similar experiences are reported by Bennett, who interviewed eight composers, one of whom said that ideas come '... like a lightning flash that you have to grab ... it has to come from the depths and you have to be listening.' (1976, 11).

The novelist Alan Sillitoe has the same experience, writing that 'I have to wait for inspiration to come. I'll sit here, looking out of the window or at maps, listening to music and then suddenly I'm off.' (Sillitoe 2007, 5). In a similar example, Wimsatt and Beardsley quote the poet A.E. Housman describing how:

> As I went along, thinking of nothing in particular, only looking at things around me and following the progress of the seasons, there would flow into my mind, with sudden and unaccountable emotion, sometimes a line or two of verse, sometimes a whole stanza at once.
>
> (1954, 8)

The poet Helen Dunmore describes how she '... wrote a poem on my phone while ... lying down a couple of days later: or rather, the poem wrote itself, unmediated by me ...' (2016). She experienced the process as if she were a passive observer. A novelist writes in a similar vein that 'A novel usually begins, in my experience, with a thought or image that won't leave me alone.' (Lanchester 2015, 13). The idea came to him and insisted on his attention. Another poet describes how the poems in her prize-winning collection '... came in what felt like an involuntary rush, and sometimes ... I felt I didn't want them, or couldn't keep up ... there was no plan.' (Benson 2019, 17). Similarly, Harold Pinter's plays often developed after a line of dialogue occurred to him. In his Nobel Prize acceptance speech, he describes how:

Most of the plays are engendered by a line, a word or an image. ... The first line of *The Homecoming* is 'What have you done with the scissors?' ... I had no further information.

(Pinter 2005, Ch. 2.)

In all these examples, ideas simply occurred to the artist. They must have arisen from subconscious reflection stimulated by experiences and the context of the artistic project concerned. In each case ideas just appeared in artists' minds as if from nowhere, rather than resulting from conscious mental effort.

These descriptions also highlight another aspect of the artistic imagination, which is reflected in composer Kaija Saariaho's description of her sense of ideas arising from the influences she has encountered. She writes that 'The material can come from our own lives, the lives around us, or wherever. But at some point, it simply becomes music.' (Saariaho 2014, no pagination). In other words, she imagines in music. Similarly, three composers included in Gabrielsson's study of what he calls 'strong' experiences of music each described how musical ideas would come to them suddenly and arrive as music (2011, 103–7). One of the composers describes having difficulties in writing a piece but how '... suddenly, creeping out from nowhere, it [the idea required] was there in my ears.' (Gabrielsson 2011, 104).

Similar experiences of imagining in music are quoted by McCutchan from her interviews with composers. Among those she interviewed, Stokes said that 'Sometimes I have to let the music take me by the hand.' (McCutchan 1999, 5); Bolcom said that 'Every piece has its own little agenda.' (McCutchan 1999, 24); Welcher spoke of being '... receptive, to think, to have experiences suggest themselves to me as potential pieces.' (McCutchan 1999, 89); and Ran said that the basic idea for an orchestral piece came to her '... while waiting at a bus stop ...' (McCutchan 1999, 119). As another of the composers, Lerdahl, put it '... the fact that I could think in sound was very mysterious to him [the composer's father].' (McCutchan 1999, 108). In a similar experience, a poet records that 'I think in poetry ...' (Sissay 2016, 6).

The two features of the imagination reflected in these descriptions are:

1. **Subconscious origin of ideas.** As suggested earlier in this chapter, ideas originate from the artists' subconscious and arise from experience. They then just pop into consciousness.
2. **Direct imagination.** Ideas arrive in the medium of the art form concerned. Artists do not decide what it is they wish to communicate

and then seek ideas in the medium of their art to communicate that meaning. As Kaschub puts it in her article on *Exercising the Musical Imagination*, 'Composition is an experience that involves thinking in sound.' (1997, 26).

Of course, there may be accounts by composers who experience their imaginative process in other ways, but I have not come across them.

Two distinct imaginative activities

As has been pointed out by several writers who studied how artists imagine, there is a difference between coming up with an idea and deciding what to do with it. This same distinction is reflected in comments made by composers. One writer, Johnson-Laird, explains that '... there are two stages in many sorts of creation: a generative stage and an evaluative stage.' (2002, 422). Ideas are first imagined. The activities of evaluation and decision-making follow, processes which are practically inseparable in the arts. If a composer imagines an idea and then evaluates it as either 'right' or 'wrong' in the context of the piece, this amounts to making a decision on whether to use, reject, or revise it.

A similar distinction is made by Finke in his comprehensive review of this subject. He proposes the 'Geneplore' model, which consists of two phases: '(1) the generative phase, in which mental representations are created; and (2) the exploratory phase, in which interpretations of the representations are explored.' (1996, 381–93). This distinction is close to Johnson-Laird's. Generation is effectively the same process as imagining, with the difference being that 'generation' implies that ideas are found through an active process of exploration and improvisation. Exploration is practically the same as evaluation and decision making.

In his book on *The creative process*, Ghiselin distinguishes three stages, writing that: 'After inspiration and conception comes execution.' (1952, 48). By inspiration, he appears to mean inward listening, and by conception, he means the emergence of ideas. Execution is then the construction of something from these ideas. I am not convinced of the value of distinguishing inward listening from the emergence of ideas since accounts of imagining rarely separate these. Execution, in his terms, is a more conscious process of working out how to use ideas. Sloboda draws a similar distinction from the accumulated evidence on how the musical imagination works and his own first-hand experience as a composer, describing a stage of inspiration when ideas arrive 'unbidden' (1999, 116) and a stage of execution when composers use their '... repertoire of ways of extending and building from the given.' (1999, 116).

The second stages identified by Ghiselin and Sloboda appear to concern the work of developing and using the ideas initially imagined. It seems to me that this must follow the evaluation of the ideas which have appeared in the artist's imagination and taking decisions on them. Until an artist feels that the ideas are right, they are likely to delay exploring or developing them further.

Further accounts by artists suggest that the distinction between these two activities, the initial imagination of ideas and their subsequent assessment, is widely experienced, and that this is only then followed by the third activity involving the more conscious working out of ideas. As an example, I referred in Chapter 1 to Konečni's description of Beethoven's imaginative process in the *Ode to Joy*, and the more than two hundred sketches he made (2012, 148). Beethoven appears to have imagined a musical idea, and then imagined many variations on this idea until he finally decided on a version which satisfied him. One part of his process was the invention of an idea. The other part was the evaluation and rejection of versions of this until he eventually settled on one which satisfied his imagination.

The same distinction is reflected in John Taverner's description of the subconscious process by which he realised that the material he had notated felt right. He says, referring to whether changes are needed, that 'Yes I can, and not only by looking at the music. It could be by looking at the cat ...' (1999, 145), and that 'When I'm composing in Greece, to walk along and sit by the sea at night or to look at the landscape somehow tells me whether I've got it right or wrong.' (1999, 145). Ghiselin quotes a similar description of the evolution of another Beethoven piece, and the way the sketches appear to reflect an eventual '... flash of recognition that this was exactly what he [Beethoven] wanted.' (1952, 47).

Novelist Henry James described a related experience of first having an idea, becoming aware that it needed working on, and returning it to his subconscious for further reflection so that he would be able to evaluate it. Ghiselin quotes him as saying:

> I was charmed with my idea, which would take, however, much working out; and precisely because it had so much to give, I think, I must have dropped it for the time into the deep well of unconscious cerebration.
>
> (1952, 26)

Just as many of Pinter's plays developed from a line of dialogue which occurred to him, he also just knew when a play was complete, in the sense that at that point he evaluated it and was satisfied. He says, 'One day I began to write *Ashes to Ashes*, and another day I knew it was complete.' (Taylor-Batty 2005, 175). A similar experience is reported by a writer who repeatedly revises his work. He writes that he knows a novel is complete because:

> somewhere between versions 15 and 25, something happens. The frisson you get when you read your words back and they seem to have been written by someone – or something – that is not quite you. A rightness like a heavy oak door clicking softly home on to its latch.
>
> (Haddon 2016, 5)

These accounts by artists, and the analyses produced by academic writers, support the idea that there are two separate activities within the subconscious imaginative process. There is general agreement that the first of the activities concerns the imagination or generation of ideas. The question is how best to characterise the second activity. I suggest that 'evaluation and decision making' is the most appropriate term for the activity which follows having or finding an idea. An artist needs at that point to allow their subconscious mind to assess the new idea to help them decide whether to use, revise, or discard it. They may also evaluate a full draft in the same way and make a decision that it is complete because they just 'know' that it is finished.

The accounts by artists suggest that this process of evaluation and decision-making is, like imagining or generating, largely subconscious. As Carroll comments, artists rarely evaluate ideas according to explicit criteria or through conscious judgement, but rather they '… typically use the language of correctness – "That's right," "It feels right," or "It clicks" – to explain their choices …' (2003, 221). Concerning the opposite sense, that an idea is not right, Adolfe describes how 'You feel that it's not what you wanted; it's not what you set out to say … it may be very good, but you no longer find it personal and an expression of what you had in mind.' (2001, 72).

The term 'execution' used by Ghiselin (1952, 48) and Sloboda (1999, 116) does not fully reflect this need to judge whether an artistic idea feels right or has potential before making use of it. It relates instead to the subsequent and more conscious activity of making art with the ideas which have been imagined and evaluated.

The two generic activities which rely on the subconscious imaginative process can therefore best be defined as:

1. **Imagination or generation**, when ideas occur to the artist or are found by exploration.
2. **Evaluation and decision making,** when the artist realises that an idea feels right or wrong, and decides whether to accept or reject it, or to revise it further.

Of course, the subsequent work to apply and explore an idea may involve the imagination and evaluation of developments and variations of the initial idea, and the imagination and evaluation of further ideas which seem necessary as work proceeds. As a result, these two activities will not simply take place sequentially, since there will be a constant shift between imagining ideas, evaluating them, working out how to use them, and imagining and evaluating new ideas or alternatives.

Both of these activities appear to be rooted in the subconscious imagination. Ideas initially arise from subconscious reflection and are then judged in terms of a subconscious sense of 'rightness'. The artist just knows that an idea is right, or a piece is finished.

Conclusion

My aim here has been to develop a more precise statement of a frequently expressed view of the operation of the imagination. This is that ideas arise from a dialogue provoked by active engagement with the environment and that this dialogue takes place largely in the subconscious mind. I've drawn together ideas and evidence from a wide range of studies in psychology, neurology, aesthetics, and musicology to support this conclusion. Only the drawing together has any originality.

It might be objected that, by carrying out an investigation of this type, I may remove some of the wonderful mystery from artistic creation. I am indeed trying to remove the element of mystery, though not the wonder. As with scientific explanations of natural phenomena which were not previously understood, an explanation may remove the mystery without weakening the sense of wonder at the natural world.

There are two good reasons for trying to understand how the artistic imagination works. One is that the idea of creating art might then seem less the prerogative of special individuals, and more an activity in which anyone can engage and gain a sense of fulfilment. Perkins' aim in his book is to '... show how creating in the arts and sciences is a natural comprehensible extension and orchestration of ordinary everyday abilities ...' (1981, 3). Showing this in no way detracts from the remarkable nature of great music but does make it seem more of a human than a god-like achievement.

The second reason is that an understanding of how the imagination functions could help artists produce work with which they are better pleased. If they deepen their understanding of how their imaginations work, they should be able to learn to use them more effectively, though this is not a subject on which there is space to expand in this book.

The way composers and other artists describe their imaginative processes is consistent with my suggestion on how the imagination works, and this lends credibility to the suggestion. The additional benefit of examining these descriptions is that further features of the imaginative process have come to light. One is that artistic ideas arrive in the language of the art form concerned. Composers think in music, poets in poetry, and so on. This is important to my discussion of meaning making from music in Chapter 4. The other feature is that there are two distinct activities within the subconscious imaginative process, imagining or generating ideas, and their evaluation to make decisions on them. This is the key to my discussion of collaborative work in Chapter 3.

Note

1 For further discussion of this subject see: McMaster and Wastell (2005), Barron (2003), and Harman (2014).

References

Adolfe, Bruce. 2001. "With Music in Mind." In *The Origin of Creativity*, edited by Karl H. Pfenninger & Valerie R. Shubik, 69–88. Oxford & New York: Oxford University Press.

Bailes, Freya, & Laura Bishop. 2012. "Musical Imagery in the Creative Process." In *The Act of Musical Composition*, edited by Dave Collins, 53–79. Farnham & Burlington VT: Ashgate.

Bakhtin, Mikhail. 1981. *The Dialogic Imagination*. Translated by Caryl Emerson & Michael Holquist. Austin: University of Texas Press.

Barron, Colin. 2003. "A Strong Distinction Between Humans and Non-Humans is no Longer Required for Research Purposes: A Debate Between Bruno Latour and Steve Fuller." *History of the Human Sciences* 16 (2): 77–99. doi.org/10.1177/0952695103016002004

Beard, Alex. 2017. *Natural Born Learners*. London: Weidenfeld & Nicholson.

Bennett, Stan. 1976. "The process of Musical Creation: Interviews with Eight Composers." *Journal of Research in Music Education* 24: 3–13. DOI: 10.2307/3345061
Benson, Fiona. 2019. "Mixing Greek Myths with #MeToo Lands Poet £10,000 Forward Prize." *The Guardian.* 22 (10). Accessed 24 September 2019. www.theguardian.com/books/2019/oct/20/fiona-benson-wins-forward-prize-greek-myth-poems-metoo
Blacking, John. 1971. *How Musical is Man?* Seattle and London: University of Washington Press. DOI: 10.21504/amj.v5i3.1669
Buzsáki, György. 2019. *The Brain from Inside Out.* Oxford & New York: Oxford University Press. DOI: 10.1093/oso/9780190905385.001.0001
Carroll, Noël. 2003. "Art, Creativity, and Tradition." In *The Creation of Art: New Essays in Philosophical Aesthetics*, edited by Berys Gaut & Paisley Livingstone, 208–34. Cambridge & New York: Cambridge University Press.
Cook, Nicholas. 2012. "Beyond Creativity?" In *Musical Imaginations: Multidisciplinary Perspectives on Creativity, Performance, and Perception*, edited by David J. Hargreaves, Dorothy E. Miell & Raymond A.R. MacDonald, 451–59. Oxford: Oxford University Press. DOI: 10.1093/acprof:oso/9780199568086.001.0001
Copland, Aaron. 1953. *Music and Imagination.* Cambridge, MA: Harvard University Press.
Cortese, Aurelio, Hakwan Lau & Mitsuo Kawato. 2020. "Unconscious Reinforcement Learning of Hidden Brain States Supported by Confidence." *Nature Communications* 11: 1–8. doi.org/10.1038/s41467-020-17828-8
Crawford, Cassandra S. 2004. "Actor Network Theory." *Ritzer-Encyclopedia,* 7/14/2004. www.sagepub.com/sites/default/files/upm-binaries/5222_Ritzer__Entries_beginning_with_A__[1].pdf. Accessed 26 August 2020.
Damasio, Antonio. 2001. "Some Notes on Brain, Imagination and Creativity." In *The Origin of Creativity*, edited by Karl H. Pfenninger & Valerie R. Shubik, 59–68. Oxford & New York: Oxford University Press.
———. 2006. *Descartes' Error: Emotion, Reason and the Human Brain.* London: Vintage Books.
———. 2018. *The Strange Order of Things.* New York: Pantheon Books.
Delalande, François. 2007. *Towards an Analysis of Compositional Strategies.* Accessed 15 March 2016. id.erudit.org/iderudit/016771ar. DOI: 10.7202/016771ar
Deleuze, Gilles and Felix Guattari. 2016. *A Thousand Plateaus.* Translated by Brian Massumi. London: Bloomsbury Academic.
Descartes, René. 1970. *The Philosophical Works of Descartes,* edited by Elizabeth S. Haldane & R.T. Ross. Vol 1. Cambridge: Cambridge University Press.
Dewey, John. 1933. *How We Think: A Restatement of the Relation of Reflective Thinking to the Educative Process.* Boston: Heath.
Donin, Nicolas & François-Xavier Féron. 2012. "Tracking the Composer's Cognition in the Course of a Creative Process: Stefano Gervasoni and the Beginning of Gramiga." *Musicae Scientiae* 16 (3): 262–85. DOI: 10.1177/1029864912448328

Donin, Nicolas & Jacques Thereau. 2007. "Theoretical and Methodological Issues Related to Long Term Creative Cognition: The Case of Musical Composition." *Cognition, Technology & Work* 9 (4): 233–51. DOI: 10.1007/s10111-007-0082-z

Donin, Nicolas. 2017. "Domesticating Gesture: The Collaborative Creative Process of Florence Baschet's Streicherskreis for Augmented String Quartet (2006–8)." In *Distributed Creativity: Collaboration and Improvisation in Contemporary Music*, edited by Eric F. Clarke & Mark Doffman, 70–87. Oxford: Oxford University Press. DOI: 10.1093/oso/9780199355914.001.0001

Donnellan, Ed, Colin Bannard, Michelle L. McGillion, Katie E. Slocombe, & Danielle Matthews. 2019. "Infants' Intentionally Communicative Vocalizations Elicit Responses from Caregivers and are the Best Predictors of the Transition to Language: A Longitudinal Investigation of Infants' Vocalizations, Gestures and Word Production." *Developmental Science* 23 (1). DOI: 10.1111/desc.12843

Dunmore, Helen. 2016. "My Working Day." *The Guardian Review*, 20 (8): 5. www.theguardian.com/books/2016/aug/20/helen-dunmore-my-writing-day

Empson, William. 1930. *Seven Types of Ambiguity*. London: Chatto & Windus.

Ericsson, K. Anders & Herbert A. Simon. 1984. *Protocol Analysis: Verbal Reports as Data*. Cambridge MA & London: The MIT Press.

Fernyhough, Charles. 2016. *The Voices Within*. London: Profile Books.

Finke, Ronald. 1996. "Imagery, Creativity and Emergent Structure." *Consciousness and Cognition* 5 (3): 381–93. DOI: 10.1006/ccog.1996.0024

Fontaine, Sheryl I. & Susan M. Hunter. 2006. *Collaborative Writing in Composition Studies*. Boston MA and London: Thomson Wadsworth.

Gabrielsson, Alf. 2011. *Strong Experiences with Music: Music is Much More Than Just Music*. Oxford & New York: Oxford University Press. DOI:10.1093/acprof:oso/9780199695225.001.0001

Ghiselin, Brewster. 1952. "The Creative Process: A Symposium." Berkeley CA: University of California Press.

Glazner, Nancy. 2001. "Dialogic Subversion: Bakhtin, the Novel and Gertrude Stein." In *Bakhtin and Cultural Theory*, edited by Ken Shepherd & David Hirschkop, 155–76. Manchester: Manchester University Press.

Godøy, Rolf I. 2010. "Gestural Affordances of Musical Sound." In *Musical Gestures: Sound, Movement, and Meaning*, edited by Rolf I. Godøy & Marc Leman, 103–25. New York & Abingdon: Routledge.

Godøy, Rolf I., Egil Haga & Alexander R. Jensenius. 2005. "Playing "Air Instruments": Mimicry of Sound-Producing Gestures by Novices and Experts". Gesture in Human-Computer Interaction and Simulation, 6th International Gesture Workshop, Berder Island, France.

Haueisen, Jens & Thomas R. Knösche. 2001. "Involuntary Motor Activity in Pianists Evoked by Music Perception." *Journal of Cognitive Neuroscience* 13 (6): 786–92. DOI: 10.1162/08989290152541449

Guimaraes Lima, Marcelo. 1995. "From Aesthetics to Psychology: Notes on Vygotsky's Psychology of Art." *Anthropology and Education Quarterly* 26 (4): 410–24. DOI: aeq.1995.26.4.05x1061u

Haddon, Mark. 2016. "My Working Day." *The Guardian Review* 7 (7): 5. www.theguardian.com/books/2016/jul/23/my-writing-day-mark-haddon

Hamburger, Michael. 1992. *Beethoven: Letters, Journals and Conversation.* New York: Thames & Hudson.

Hargreaves, David J., Dorothy E. Miell, & Raymond A.R. MacDonald. 2012. *Musical Imaginations: Multidisciplinary Perspectives on Creativity, Performance, and Perception.* Oxford & New York: Oxford University Press. DOI: 10.1093/acprof:oso/9780199568086.001.0001

Harman, Graham. 2014. "Entanglement and Relation: A Response to Bruno Latour and Ian Hodder." New Literary History 45 (1) 37–49. DOI: 10.1353/nlh.2014.0007

Hermans, Hubert J.M. & Harry J.G. Kempen. 1993. *The Dialogical Self: Meaning as Movement.* San Diego CA: Academic Press.

Holquist, Michael. 1981. "Introduction." In *The Dialogic Imagination*, by Mikhail Bakhtin. Austin TX: University of Texas Press.

James, William. 1890. *The Principles of Psychology, Vol. 1.* London: Macmillan.

Johnson-Laird, P.N. 2002. "How Jazz Musicians Improvise." *Music Perception* 19 (3): 415–42. DOI: 10.1525/mp.2002.19.3.415

Kaschub, Michele. 1997. "Exercising the Musical Imagination." *Music Educators Journal* 84 (3): 26–32. DOI: 10.2307/3399053

Kipnis, Andrew B. 2015 "Agency Between Humanism and Posthumanism: Latour and his Opponents." *Journal of Ethnographic Theory* 5 (2): 43–58. DOI: dx.doi.org/10.14318/hau5.2.004

Konečni, Vladimir J. 2012. "'Composers' Creative Process: The Role of Life-Events, Emotion and Reason." In *Musical Imaginations: Multidisciplinary Perspectives on Creativity, Performance, and Perception*, edited by David J. Hargreaves, Dorothy E. Miell & Raymond A.R. MacDonald, 141–55. Oxford: Oxford University Press. DOI: 10.1093/acprof:oso/9780199568086.001.0001

Kounios, John & Mark Beeman. 2015. *The Eureka Factor: Creative Insights and the Brain.* London: Windmill Books.

Kuhl, Patricia K., Feng-Ming Tsao, & Huei-Mei Liu. 2003. "Foreign Language Experience in Infancy: Effects of Short-Term Exposure and Social Interaction on Phonetic Learning." *Proceedings of the National Academy of Sciences of the United States* 100 (15): 9096–101. DOI: 10.1073/pnas.1532872100

Lanchester, John. 2015. "Capital." *The Guardian Review* 21 (11): 13.

Latour, Bruno. 1996. "On Actor-Network Theory. A Few Clarifications, Plus More Than a Few Complications." *Soziale Welt* 47: 369–81.

Leman, Marc. 2008. *Embodied Music Cognition and Mediation Technology.* Cambridge MA: The MIT Press.

Mahn, Holbrook & Vera John-Steiner. 2002. "The Gift of Confidence: A Vygotskian View of Emotions." In *Learning for Life in the 21st Century: Sociocultural Perspectives on the Future of Education*, edited by Gordon Wells & Guy Claxton, 46–58. Oxford: Blackwell.

McCutchan, Ann. 1999. *The Muse that Sings: Composers Speak About the Creative Process*. Oxford: Oxford University Press.

McMaster, Tom & David Wastell. 2005. "The Agency of Hybrids: Overcoming the Symmetrophobic Block." *Scandinavian Journal of Information Systems* 17 (1): 175–82. OAI identifier: oai:CiteSeerX.psu:10.1.1.217.6285

Nisbett, R.E. & T.D. Wilson. 1977. "Telling More Than We Can Know: Verbal Reports on Mental Processes." *Psychology Review* 84: 239–59. DOI: 10.1037//0033-295X.84.3.231

Noordhof, Paul. 2008. "Expressive Perception as Projective Imagining." *Mind and Language* 329–58. DOI: 10.1111/j.1468-0017.2008.00346.x

Perkins, D.N. 1981. *The Mind's Best Work*. Cambridge MA: Harvard University Press.

Piaget, Jean. 1967. *Biologie et Connasisance. Essai sur les Relations Entre les Régulations Organiques et les Processus Cognitifs*. Paris: Gallimand.

Pinter, Harold. 2005. *Nobel Lecture: Art, Truth & Politics*. Accessed 02 January 2017. www.nobelprize.org/nobel_prizes/literature/laureates/2005/pinter-lecture-e.html

Plato. 2016. *Apology: The Apology of Socrates*. Cabin John MD: Wildside Press.

Predota, George. 2019. *How Inspiration Strikes*. Accessed 07 May 2019. www.interlude.hk/front/inspiration-strikes/

Reybrouck, Mark M. 2006. "Musical Creativity between Symbolic Modelling and Perceptual Constraints: The Role of Adaptive Behaviour and Epistemic Autonomy." In *Musical Creativity: Multidisciplinary Research in Theory and Practice*, edited by Irène Deliège & Geraint A. Wiggins, 42–59. Hove & New York: Psychology Press.

Saariaho, Kaija. 2014. *A Conversation with Kajia Saariaho; Interview with Clément Mao-Takas*. 9. Accessed 19 June 2017. www.musicandliterature.org/features/2014/9/22/a-conversation-with-kaija-saariaho

Shepherd, David. 2001. "Bakhtin and the Reader." In *Bakhtin and Cultural Theory*, edited by Ken Hirschkop & David Shepherd, 136–54. Manchester: Manchester University Press.

Sillitoe, Alan. 2007. *The Loneliness of the Long Distance Runner*. London & New York: Harper Perennial.

Sissay, Lemn. 2016. "My Working Day." *The Guardian Review* 10 (09): 6.

Sloboda, John. 1999. *The Musical Mind: The Cognitive Psychology of Music*. Oxford & New York: OUP. DOI: 10.1093/acprof:oso/9780198521280.001.0001

Small, Christopher. 1998. *Musicking: The Meanings of Performing and Listening*. Middletown CT: Wesleyan University Press.

Taverner, John. 1999. *The Music of Silence: A Composer's Testament*. London: Faber & Faber.

Taylor-Batty, Mark. 2005. *About Pinter: The Playwright and the Work*. London: Faber and Faber.

Tchaikovsky, Modeste. 2004. *The Life and Letters of Peter Ilich Tchaikovsky*. Honolulu: University Press of the Pacific.

The Bible, Authorized Version. 1957. I Kings 19:12. London: The British and Foreign Bible Society.

Vygotsky, Lev S. 1978. *Mind in Society: The Development of Higher Psychological Processes*. Cambridge MA: Harvard University Press.
Wiggins, Geraint A. 2012. "The Mind's Chorus: Creativity Before Consciousness." *Cognitive Computing* 4: 306–19. DOI: 10.1007/s12559-012-9151-6
Wimsatt, William K. & Monroe C. Beardsley. 1954. "The Intentional Fallacy." In *The Verbal Icon: Studies in the Meaning of Poetry*, edited by William K. Wimsatt, 3–20. Lexington: University of Kentucky Press.

3 Sharing imaginations[1]

Introduction

Artistic collaboration and the sharing of imaginative work are common, though more common in some arts and some types of music than in others. They are fundamental to jazz improvisation of course, while Bennett (2012) describes cases of the joint writing of pop songs (2012) and Fontaine and Hunter list examples of shared literary writing (2006, 107–26). Dancers also invent moves together. However, I've come across no examples of shared invention in the visual arts, only cases of pupils filling in backgrounds after a master has completed the main part of a painting or assistants constructing pieces supervised by the lead artist.

There must be differences between these arts which affect the ability of their practitioners to invent together. As Moran and John-Steiner explain, '… collaborators' inner speech – their condensed stream of thought that generates creative associations … must be shared.' (2004, 15). The question for any artists working together will be how to share this subconscious thought process, and this is likely to be easier in some arts than in others. How are painters to communicate about the exact type of brushstroke or tint of colour to use when painting, for instance? By contrast, the invention of dance moves can be shared through moving together.

Due to this need to communicate, artists are likely to encounter limits to their ability to share imaginative work. It is too easy to assume that work will proceed as if working on one's own when in fact there will be a need to adjust to working and communicating with partners. For instance, composer John Adams worked successfully with many artists, particularly his long-term collaborator, director Peter Sellers. He still found this a challenge, and comments that '… next to double murder-suicide, it [artistic collaboration] might be the most painful thing two people can do together.' (2008, 221–2). His experience should be a warning that artistic collaboration requires skill and mutual understanding.

My aim in this chapter is to analyse the ways in which imaginative work can be shared and to propose a typology of ways of working which could help artists overcome some of the obstacles to success. I showed in Chapter 2 that there are two separate activities within imaginative work, imagining or generating ideas, and evaluating them to take decisions. The question in shared working will be whether one, the other, both, or neither of these activities can be shared, and so, in these terms at least, there must be four different ways of sharing imaginative work.

This brings me to composed music, the main focus of my discussion. Just as with the imagination, it represents a good subject for testing ideas on shared imaginative working, since it is not immediately obvious how a composer could share the process of deciding which notes to write. To discuss this with a partner, maybe a performer or another composer, would be impractical for anything beyond short passages. It would also risk replacing the subconscious activities of imagining and evaluating ideas with more explicit judgemental processes.

Composers do often ask artists they are working with for suggestions, or for their opinion on musical sketches, but they rarely share their creative process more fully. There must be reasons for this which do not apply to jazz or many other forms of improvised music. Contrasts of this type are the subject of this chapter, and they exist due to variations in the constraints on the ability to share the imagination and evaluation of ideas between different art forms and musical genres.

There will, of course, be non-human 'third parties' in any artistic collaboration, for instance musical instruments. I discussed the debate around the relationship between the human and non-human in the previous chapter and took the view, following Kipnis (2015), that they are not equivalents since humans have intentions whereas non-living things do not. A composer and their artistic partners come to a collaboration with preferences and make choices as they work together. A musical instrument, or any specific notation system, will offer possibilities and impose limitations due to its inherent nature, but it does not have intentions or make choices. For that reason, my focus in this chapter will be on the nature, and variety, of the imaginative interchanges between the people involved.

The misuse of the term 'collaboration'

The first step in this discussion, however, must be to untangle some of what seems to me the confusion or, at least, the obscuring of important distinctions, caused by the use of 'collaboration' as an umbrella term for many different ways of working. As Dillenbourg writes, 'When a word becomes fashionable – as is the case with "collaboration" – it is often used abusively for more or less anything.' (1999, 1).

As a synonym for 'influenced by'

One way in which collaboration has been used, or misused, is as a synonym for 'influenced by'. Miell and Littleton, for example, refer to '... the essentially collaborative nature of all creative endeavour.' (2004, 2) while Fontaine and Hunter comment that '... all writing is, by its very nature, a collaborative activity, that it is social and naturally includes other people and other writers.' (2006, 312).

The problem with this usage is that there are important differences between creating alone affected by conscious and subconscious influences and sharing creative work with others present and actively involved. To give an example of the way different kinds of imaginative working have been grouped together under this umbrella term, Mercer lists the Brontës, the Lakes Poets, The Beatles, and the Impressionists as examples of collaboration (2000, 3). However, there is surely a difference between Lennon and McCartney writing a song together and Wordsworth and Coleridge working alongside each other on their separate poems to be published in their *Lyrical Ballads* (2007). The Impressionists were in contact with one another but worked alone on their paintings. The Brontë sisters certainly commented on one another's writing but did not rewrite together. As Ellis, writing about Anne, explains 'Every night, she and her sisters paced round and round the dining table, reading their work aloud and offering criticism and ideas.' (2017, 16). However, they did not sit together and rewrite but decided separately how to react to their sisters' suggestions.

There seem to be three contrasting patterns of working here, and these differences are obscured if they are all described as collaborations. Lennon and McCartney shared writing songs and shared all or most of the work on each song which they co-wrote. The Brontës asked each other's opinion on their work but then worked alone to make revisions. The Impressionists, and Wordsworth and Coleridge, discussed the aesthetic ideas which informed their breaks with tradition but then worked alone, though influenced by their friends.

Artists working alone but influenced by each other and their environment – influences which are always and unavoidably present – do not need to find a way of sharing the activities of imagining and evaluating ideas. The fact that artists never truly imagine alone, but are always

Sharing imaginations 57

influenced by other people, is an aspect of the distributed creativity fundamental to the production of any art. Now that this term is widely accepted, it would be best to avoid using 'collaboration' to describe the way artists are always influenced by other people.

As a synonym for 'working together'

Even when artists do work together directly, they may work in one of several contrasting ways, and it is potentially confusing to label all of these as collaborations. Dobson describes this problem, writing that:

> When discussing collaboration we could be talking about anything from independent parallel working, characterised most extremely by [composer John] Cage and [choreographer Merce] Cunningham's work, by cooperation where each member of a group performs a distinct role independently, or a much more involved approach perhaps seen when musicians improvise and perform Jazz.
>
> (Dobson 2009, 6)

A study of groups of arts students illustrates the effect of calling all forms of shared working 'collaborations'. The researcher follows this practice but notes that '... some groups naturally developed systems in which each member was primarily responsible for a different technical or artistic aspect of the project, while other groups tended to work out all aspects collectively.' (C. Watts 2004, 297). Similarly, Gall and Breeze describe how, in the 'collaborations' they studied, '... practice between the pairs of students varied between taking charge of different sections of the music, to agreeing every part of it.' (2008, 34). The various student teams studied by these writers clearly worked in contrasting ways, and this would have been easier to describe had there been different terms for these.

If all kinds of shared working are described as collaborations in this way, artists are less likely to think critically about how they and their partners are working or to explore alternatives. They may also find that misunderstandings develop since the partners could be making conflicting assumptions about how the relationship is expected to work. This exact problem was found by John Adams. He had a difficult working relationship with the librettist of the opera *I Was Looking at the Ceiling and Then I Saw the Sky*. She was a well-established writer and a specialist in the subject matter of the opera. Adams assumed that, as with his other operas, the writer would produce a libretto and he would be free to change words where necessary in setting them to music (2008, 222). The writer assumed that they were equal partners, and objected to Adams altering the words (2008, 220).

There are other well-established terms for shared working apart from collaboration, such as co-operation and consultation. Defining these, and contrasting them with collaboration defined more tightly, could help people sharing imaginative work to understand, and perhaps to change or adapt, the ways in which they are working. Certainly, it is best to be clear about the nature of the relationship at the start of any shared working to avoid problems developing later, and this would be helped by having clearly-defined terms for contrasting forms of working.

Suggestions for better definitions

The fact that there is a problem with the terminology used for shared working is reflected in the way several writers have proposed different definitions for the contrasting forms they identify. One approach has been to define different kinds of collaboration. For instance, Hankinson and O'Grady suggest that:

> there are basically two methods of collaboration: one in which the individuals work separately, bringing the results of their labor together at the end of the process, and a second in which the individuals work together, presenting ideas and feedback on ideas in a constant flow until a final product is mutually agreed upon.
> (1981, 202)

Another distinction is drawn by John-Steiner, based on her study of pairs of artists such as Picasso and Braque (John-Steiner 2000, 65–70) and Stravinsky and Balanchine (John-Steiner 2000, 93–4). She identifies two different forms of collaboration. In the first type, artists share imaginative work on artistic concepts before working on their separate pieces, while in the second they divide work on a single project between them.

The problem with these distinctions is that the contrasting types of 'collaboration' identified differ in kind, not in degree. They are not on a scale from close to more distant; rather, the relationships described worked in quite different ways from one another, and so it would be more logical to have distinct terms for these contrasting ways of working.

One suggestion proposed by composers Hayden and Windsor, and based on their own work with performers, is that there are three types of relationship. They suggest a tighter definition of collaboration for one of them and propose different terms for the other two. The types are:

1. Directive: in which there is a hierarchy and the composer instructs the performers.
2. Interactive: in which there is a negotiation between the partners, '... but ultimately, the composer is still the author.'
3. Collaborative: in which '... the development of the music is achieved by a group through a collective decision-making process.' (2007, 33).

In the first two types of relationship, there is a decision-making hierarchy with the composer making the decisions. The difference between the two is that in the second, interactive or consultative type, the performers and the composer all suggest ideas but the composer evaluates them. In the cases they describe as collaborative, all participants both suggest and evaluate ideas.

A separate distinction, between co-operation and collaboration, is drawn by Dillenbourg, and by John-Steiner in an earlier contribution. They describe tasks as being divided between participants in co-operation but shared in collaboration. John-Steiner describes how, in co-operative relationships, the partners '... each make specific contributions to a shared task ...' (1997, 12), whereas in collaborative relationships '... participants see themselves engaged in a joint task ...' (1999, 13). Dillenbourg draws the same distinction, writing that 'In co-operation, partners split the work, solve sub-tasks "individually" and then assemble the partial results into the final output. In collaboration, partners work "together".' (1999, 11).

Going back to first principles – four types of working relationships

There is clearly a problem with the terminology on this subject, but there does not yet seem to be a generally accepted set of terms for different types of shared working. For this reason I suggest a different approach, which is to go back to first principles and ask what it is that leads artists to work in one way or in another contrasting way.

I suggested at the end of the previous chapter that there are two separate activities within imaginative work. These will be the activities which artists may find it hardest to share simply because they rely on the subconscious. The questions for artists working together will therefore be:

1. Whether or not they can share imagining or generating ideas.
2. Separately, whether or not they can share evaluating ideas and take decisions on them.

Partners might share both, only one, only the other, or neither of these activities. In these terms at least, there must be four distinct ways in which artists can work together. Defining these different ways would make it possible to distinguish between them clearly, and so help artists to gain a better understanding of how they might share their work. In the table I suggest terms for them, three of which are well known and understood, and the fourth is a tighter definition of collaboration.

These definitions correspond with proposals made by other writers:

- Co-operation is defined in the same way by John-Steiner (1997, 12) and Dillenbourg (1999, 11).
- Consultation is defined in this way by Hayden and Windsor, who call it integrative working (2007, 33).
- The tighter definition of collaboration corresponds with the definitions proposed by John-Steiner (1997, 12) and Dillenbourg (1999, 70).
- Hierarchical working corresponds with Hayden and Windsor's 'directive' type (2007, 33).

As in the case of my proposed view of the working of the imagination, I have drawn these separate threads together into what I hope is a neater and more helpful pattern. I have also shown that these different types of shared working result from the underlying constraint of whether or not artists find they can share the two essentially subconscious activities of imagining or generating ideas and evaluating them to make decisions.

Table 3.1 Types of working relationship

		Is the evaluation of, and decision making on, ideas shared?	
		No	Yes
Is the imagination or generation of ideas shared?	No	**Hierarchical working** People imagine ideas for separate parts of the project. One person evaluates them.	**Co-operative working** People imagine ideas for separate parts of the project. Evaluation is shared and equal.
	Yes	**Consultative working** People imagine ideas for the same part of the project. One person evaluates them.	**Collaborative working** People share imagining ideas, and evaluating them, as equals.

Within this framework, co-operative relationships might also take one of two different forms:

1. Where there is an agreed concept or scenario, perhaps produced collaboratively, and the partners then make their contributions separately but as equals. In some cases, the partners might compare and discuss their contributions, while in others they might accept that their partner's contribution will follow the agreed concept without the need for further discussion. This could be called pre-planned co-operation.
2. Where the partners work alongside each other on their separate contributions, sharing decisions as they go along. This could be called interactive co-operation.

Three questions need to be answered about these proposed types of working relationships. One concerns whether they can be used to describe all the ways in which artists work together or whether there are intermediate types between them not covered by these four terms. This can be tested by analysing some examples of shared working in composition. The second is whether the types concern just the mechanics of the relationships or are also experienced in different ways. The third concerns the language of communication which artists use when they share creative work, and whether this affects the form taken by their shared working.

Are there intermediate types of working?

I previously analysed 95 published examples of composers working with other artists (2018) and found that the way they worked with their partners could always be characterised accurately using one or other of these four types of relationship, and so I doubt whether there are intermediate types. This finding can be illustrated by describing in detail some examples of shared working of composers with musical performers and choreographers.

In each of these cases, there were of course 'third parties' involved such as musical instruments, and also other people such as performers not actively involved in the initial imagination of the project. However, my focus in this chapter is on the interaction between the imaginative processes of the central artistic partners and the ways in which they shared their work, so I will pay less attention to these other elements.

Performers

John Harbison's relationship with the soloist for whom he wrote his oboe concerto is a typical example of composer–performer working. Fronckowiak describes how 'Bennett's [the soloist's] suggestions, personality, and playing style influenced Harbison's writing' (2006, 3). She reports that their 'discussions' took place by post, with Bennett playing through sketches and mailing back recordings and comments. These included discussion of certain sections he found difficult and the alternatives he suggested (2006, 8–9).

This is an example of consultative working. The composer thought of the soloist when writing and asked for comments and suggestions, which he then decided whether or not to incorporate. This appears to have led to a deeper interaction at some points, when their working was on the brink of becoming collaborative, with decisions on notational changes taken together.

Work on David Gorton's piece *Forlorn Hope* for 11-string guitar (See Gorton & Östersjö (2016) and Clarke, Doffman, Gorton & Östersjö (2017)) began with Gorton proposing some tuning systems for the instrument. The partners then worked together to explore these and generate ideas. This period of joint exploration and invention was extended and intensive, and they shared it as equals. Ideas were generated by the guitarist, Östersjö, a process closely integrated with the shared evaluation and selection of ideas. Gorton then made structural decisions about the piece on his own and wrote a score requiring the performer to make choices on the order in which to perform the different sections of the piece. The stages of their working were:

- An initial mutual exploration of possibilities, with each consulting the other on ideas and possible tunings.
- The collaborative development of a concept and approach, and the choice of a piece by the Elizabethan composer John Dowland as a model since there was a Dowland piece on the programme for the first performance, and from this the generation of possible musical ideas for the piece and their shared evaluation.
- The composer then working alone to write the score using ideas generated together.
- Refinement and adjustment through rehearsal, a form of consultation in which the composer took decisions on changes (2017, 129–30).

While their working pattern was fluid, and changed frequently from one mode or working to another, they appear to have always related to one another in just one of the ways I suggest in the table at any point in their working.

Liza Lim is a composer and academic who focusses on collaborative and transcultural practices (Lim 2020). The composition of her piece, *Tongue of the Invisible*, is analysed by Clarke, Doffman & Lim (2013). Lim began by analysing phrases from Sufi poetry and developed a series of different strategies by which performers could play music relating to the phrases. These range from forms of improvisation to sections composed in detail. Many of these were worked out with the ensemble in rehearsal.

The overall concepts for the piece, the use of Sufi poetry and the strategies for deriving music, were Lim's, and she then worked closely with the performers to find ways of using these to generate music. Some parts of the resulting piece are fully composed, while others consist of structures to be used for improvisation in performance. Lim took the decisions on the ordering of the sections and composed the parts which are fully notated. The overall concept was therefore Lim's, but she consulted the performers in developing musical ideas (2013, 661) before working alone to write a score.

Heather Roche describes her work with several composers on new pieces for clarinet (2011). She worked particularly closely with one of them, spending nearly a year developing a piece. She describes how:

> Hall [the composer] had two very different ideas for the direction the piece would take, and we spent an hour discussing these two options with the idea that I would help him to decide.
> (Roche 2011, 64)

In other words, she saw herself as being consulted. She goes on to describe how they then began a dialogue on the central idea, which led to agreement. Since they shared evaluation and decision making in agreeing this concept, I would describe this as collaboration. Hall next began to develop sketches for the piece, consulting Roche on special effects as they worked together on technical questions. Finally, he wrote a draft score and consulted her on this (Roche 2011, 80–2).

Choreographers

Work on the ballet *Appalachian Spring* was initiated by choreographer Martha Graham, who produced several provisional scripts which composer Aaron Copland either rejected or revised. Copland then wrote thematic sketches and sent Graham a piano score which had a good deal of independence from the script. Graham could read music well, and she then revised her script (Robertson 1991, 8). Their working process was, therefore, dialectic, since they arrived at this collaboratively-agreed script through a process of proposal and response until they were agreed. Their work on the script concluded when they both accepted it, although initially Graham was consulting Copland. Copland responded by suggesting different versions and eventually they agreed. They then produced the full score and choreography separately within the context of the agreed script – pre-planned co-operative working. A similar account of their work is given by Bentley (1981).

In working on their dance pieces, John Cage and Merce Cunningham chose not to co-ordinate the music and dance, but agreed that there should be no detailed relationship between them with the two taking place in the same space and over the same time-span. They collaborated to develop this shared aesthetic, and a system for the timing of sections in each piece to permit the music and dance to come together at specific points (Hodgins 1992, 17). A similar account is given by Cage and Retallack (1996), who describe how the separate compositional and choreographic work followed the collaborative development of this approach – an example of pre-planned co-operation. Cunningham himself comments that:

> What we have done is to bring together three separate elements in time and space, the music, the dance, and the décor, allowing each to remain independent.
>
> (Cunningham 1999, 137)

The pattern of Cunningham's work with Cage was, however, essentially the same as that between Graham and Copland. Each pair of partners began with the collaborative development of a shared concept, in the case of Graham and Copland a scenario, and in the case of Cunningham and Cage an aesthetic attitude and a plan for the timing of the sections of each piece. In both cases, music and choreography were then created separately. Cunningham and Cage were distinctive in working on these in parallel, with the relationship between the dance and music being one of consistency of aesthetic and section timings rather than detailed integration.

The work of composer Paul Hindemith and choreographer and dancer Léonide Massine on the Ballet *St. Francis* began with a joint visit to the basilica in Assisi. Hastings records that:

> After viewing these moving frescos [of the life of St. Francis] together, the composer and the choreographer selected episodes

that seemed appropriate for the ballet they began to plan. Massine described his vision of each scene, and Hindemith made notes and then began to play the piano ...

(1983, 120)

The process of developing the scenario based on the frescos was collaborative. Hindemith then improvised music in response to Massine's verbal description of the dramatic and choreographic action. This was a process of interactive co-operation in which they were stimulated by one another. The subsequent production of the full score and the choreography followed; another example of pre-planned co-operation in the context of a collaboratively agreed scenario.

Heisler describes the work of composer Richard Strauss on the ballet *The Legend of Joseph*. Strauss was unhappy with the religiosity of the story and sought to subvert this in his music (2009, 50). Massine was again the choreographer and lead dancer, but his working relationship with Strauss was not close. Heisler reports that:

Massine's dancing undermined the collaborator's initial vision of Joseph as set down by Hofmannsthal and Kessler [the writers of the scenario]; at the same time, Massine's performance was complicated by Strauss's music for Joseph, and vice versa.

(2009, 52)

The production process for the scenario was hierarchical, and the writers appear to have produced this without the involvement of Strauss or Massine. As a result, I suggest, these two artists developed conflicting views of the piece. The lack of collaborative working at the start to agree a scenario appears to have made it hard for them to co-operate effectively in producing their separate contributions. The ballet was not regarded as a success (Heisler 2009, 65).

Implications

I've described these examples in detail as a way of testing whether the working relationships found can be accurately described using the terms I suggest, and to establish whether the terms are helpful in analysing the shared working concerned. In these cases, the terms do help in clarifying and understanding the nature of the shared working and how this evolved as the projects progressed.

There is also no evidence of intermediate forms of working between the four I suggest. In every case, the artists shared imagining ideas or divided this between them. They also either shared the evaluation of ideas and deciding how to use them, or one person made the decisions. There were usually changes in the working pattern during the projects, but no evidence of intermediate types of working. For instance, the development of a concept for a piece might be shared, but the partners would then create the separate parts of the piece. Alternatively, a composer might develop ideas with others, but then take decisions on these ideas when working alone to write a score. While the type of working frequently changed in these ways as projects progressed, every form of working used can be classified as one or other of the types defined in the table.

The experience of different types of working

This may seem too mechanical – four types, and four types only, of relationship in imaginative work. People sharing their work in one way, or another, commonly changing how they worked, but never working in alternative or intermediate ways. However, the suggestion that there are just these four types of working does represent a form of consensus view since it is based on distinctions drawn by other writers. It is also rooted in the two basic activities within imaginative work.

It is also likely that these types may reflect not only the outward form of the relationships but also the inner experience of working in one way as opposed to another. In particular, writers have identified two key aspects of the experience of collaborative working. These are a sense of relaxation, creative empathy, and exhilaration, and that the meanings created are the work of a third or separate person.

On the first point, jazz improvisation has been described as leading to '... extreme feelings of relaxation that increase powers of expression and imagination ...' (Seddon 2004, 65). The musicians are described as experiencing an '... altered state of mind ...' (Seddon 2004, 76).

An example of the second experience of collaboration is found in the work of novelists Ford Maddox Ford and Joseph Conrad. They wrote stories jointly, and in a reported conversation '... he [Ford Maddox Ford] recalls Conrad interrupting him as he's reading their [joint] work aloud: 'By Jove' he [Conrad] said, 'it's a third person who is writing'.' (Saunders 2006, 96). Conrad felt that the story was by someone other than either of the two of them. New meanings had been created which would not have been arrived at by either partner working alone. This sense that the outcome is not the creation of any one of the participants is also described by Roche. Her own experience of working with composers is that 'One listens to gain understanding, to create a synthesis of ideas, to create the aforementioned shared voice.' (2011, 13). Fontaine and Hunter, similarly, describe how writing together can lead to the '... the shared creation of new meanings.' (2006, xxv).

These accounts suggest that the four types of relationship concern not only the mechanics of sharing imaginative work but also affect how they are experienced. Partners who are collaborating in the sense I define it would not have the experiences described above if imagining or generating ideas, and evaluating and deciding on them, were not shared. Similarly, in a co-operative working relationship, it is likely in that an artist will find a sense of satisfaction in working with a partner of equal competence and a compatible outlook to themselves, and that this stimulates their own imagination. In a consultative working relationship, the lead artist may be provoked and encouraged by the suggestions made by others and may enjoy incorporating their suggestions and finding solutions to problems they identify. The people being consulted may be pleased to be asked for their ideas and encouraged if their suggestions are adopted.

The need for a language of communication

Sharing imaginative work depends on the ability of partners to communicate. I quoted Moran and John-Steiner at the start of the chapter describing the need to share '... inner speech ...' (2004, 15). In Chapter 2 I gave examples of composers imagining in music, poets thinking in poetry, and Harold Pinter thinking in dialogue. Since artists appear to imagine in the language of their art, their ability to share their imaginative processes will clearly depend on whether they can communicate in the 'language' in which they are imagining.

As I noted at the start of the chapter, jazz improvisers communicate through hearing and inventing material in a musical idiom with which they are familiar, and dancers can communicate in the shared development of a dance through making movements. Literary writers can discuss their shared work in words and speak possible alternatives to one another. There can be a similar sense of sharing in theatre. Etchells describes the members of a theatre company who worked closely together for twelve years, achieving what he describes as '... an intimacy that approaches [that of] lovers ...' (1999, 54). The languages of the art form are spoken words and acted behaviour, and the company members could communicate in these languages when imagining without the need to translate their thoughts into a different language.

In the case of improvised jazz, dance, literary writing, and some forms of theatre, the language of the art form and the one used in communication between partners can be the same. This is not necessarily the case in other art forms and is certainly not the case in musical composition when it comes to notating musical ideas and writing out a score.

This need to communicate in a common language will become clear as soon as people attempt to share imagining or generating ideas or evaluating and deciding on them. A difference between the language in which they are inventing and the one used for communication will be a barrier to full mutual understanding. If the languages differ, then it will be necessary to 'translate' thoughts and ideas into a shared language such as words to communicate. A great deal will be lost in the translation. For example, Watts, describing poets and composers working together, describes how:

> the cross-arts encounter between a poetic text and musical environment involves for a collaborating poet and composer the exploring of a practice for which there are often no words, and indeed not always mutual understanding.
>
> (2010, 146)

The extent to which 'language' barriers will constrain the shared making of music is likely to be related to the way in which the music is made, and particularly to whether forms of musical notation are used. Most of the examples I quote in this book are of Western Art Music, and so rely on the conventions of Western musical notation. As Wishart (1996) argues, notation captures a fraction of the variability in sound possibilities in music and focusses on the ideas of fixed pitch and exact note durations. He goes on to argue that such notation represents an attempt by the scribe class to capture and control the range of musical expression, and to suppress music that is thought to be '… lascivious or morally harmful …' (1996, 15). Unfortunately, I need to avoid too long a digression by engaging with the latter argument, which seems to me to overlook the imaginative contribution of the performer in turning dry notation into something living and potentially 'lascivious', as well as notation's advantage in enabling composers to reflect on their writing, and then to revise and potentially innovate in ways which may subvert existing practice. However, the point remains that the act of codifying musical ideas in the form of musical notation presumes that the means of communication about these ideas will focus on, and be constrained by, the notation.

Collaboration, in the sense that I use the word, is common in many genres and cultures in which music is improvised. If music is invented in the act of playing, or structures are memorised and then performed with the freedom to add detail and elaboration, then the performers will be able to communicate with one another as they invent. The same is true, though in a different way, of gestural or graphic forms of musical notation, which invite performers to respond to a visual image while listening to fellow performers, rather than playing pre-specified notes or rhythms.

Western notation, similarly, has a direct effect on the way artistic partners work together since its use can act as a barrier to communication, even if all the partners read notation. When a composer seeks to capture imagined sounds through the notation, they are likely to find it hard to explain how their thoughts become notes or to share this process. This may shape the nature of their work with artistic partners and may make communication difficult. There are few examples of composers sharing the process of notating music even with other composers, and I suggest that this is the reason.

The exceptions I've found concern writing pop songs and school pupils composing together in classes. Bennett examines the working process of pairs of pop songwriters and identifies thirteen characteristics which are shared by most pop songs (2012, 142–3). The writers' ability to compose together appears to be linked to these tight constraints on the form of the songs, which result in there being a more limited range of options open to songwriters than, for instance, to contemporary music composers.

Several studies have been published of teachers telling school pupils to form groups to compose.[2] The writers describe how pupils worked together successfully when the pairs of pupils were friends, could communicate well, or when they used sound creation and editing software. This last point connects with Wishart's view that the use of computer-based composition opens up possibilities of sharing denied by the use of notation due to the ability '… to sculpt all aspects of sounds …' (Wishart 1996, 5). The pupils in the studies were told to share composing, will have tried to do so, and in some cases may have succeeded through using computer editing software. However, none of the writers describe pupils writing musical notation together in any extended way.

Adult composers rarely share writing notation with their artistic partners, even musical performers. If they tried to do so, communication with partners would depend largely on speech. Trying to talk through writing or revising notation in any extended way would be impractical. As a result, it would be difficult to establish a collaborative relationship during work on notation. The one exception I've come across, of pop songwriters sharing composing, appears to be made possible by the more limited range of compositional options available.

However, composers do frequently anticipate the process of collaboration with a specific performer, or in a sense with an instrument, writing with that performer and/or instrument in mind. This is one of several aspects of the distributed nature of creativity which I described in the previous chapter. Composers of any experience do not imagine in a vacuum, dreaming up musical ideas which are then thrust at players to make what they can of them. Rather, they think of the instrument, and often of the performer, in the act of imagining musical ideas, and certainly when working through these ideas to create musical structures.

Several examples of the integral role of performers or instruments in compositional work are given by Butt in his study of 'historically informed performance' (2002). Among these are the several versions of arias in *The Messiah* written for different soloists (2002, 90), the way Mozart specified a high degree of ornamentation in operatic arias as a way of suiting them to the style of specific singers (2002, 107–8), and the solo writing in Handel's oboe concertos which was virtuosic for the instruments of his day even though it is less difficult using modern instruments. In each case, the composer imagined and wrote thinking of the instrument or performer concerned. I suggest that any experienced composer would do the same, and therefore that the imaginative process in composition is always affected by the performers and instruments rather than being a process of abstract invention. However, in each of these cases there was no shared process of imagining or evaluating ideas, and so this form of 'anticipated' shared working falls outside the scope of this chapter.

I described at the start of the chapter how sharing imaginative work is common in the arts, and how it is normal in some arts but rare in others. It is clear from the discussion in this section that the ability to share imaginative artistic work depends on the partners' ability to communicate in the same language as the one in which they are imagining. If they can communicate in the language of the art form, they can collaborate to create art in that language. If not, they may still be able to collaborate to invent a concept for a piece using the common language of words.

Whether or not composers in the Western tradition and their partners collaborate to develop a concept for a piece, the main body of work between them has to take a different form due to the constraint on communication represented by musical notation. It is commonly the case that the composer takes the role of a lead artist who consults the others. Composers often discuss musical sketches or drafts with performers, but they rarely take decisions together. Instead, they ask for ideas or comments and take decisions by themselves – consultative working.

Another common approach is for artists to divide the work between them. This happens by necessity when composers and choreographers work together. They may first discuss a concept for a piece and often collaborate in this, but they are unable to share inventing dance or musical ideas in this way because they don't 'speak' one another's artistic languages. They, therefore, work separately on their contributions – co-operative working.

Conclusion

Since imagining or generating ideas, and evaluating and taking decisions on them, are separate activities, the key question in joint projects will be whether these two activities can be shared. Clearly, artistic partners could share one, the other, both, or neither of these activities. As a result, there are different types of shared imaginative work. An awareness of there being a series of distinct ways in which artistic partners can work together would help those involved to make a greater success of the relationship, for two reasons:

- Understanding how a relationship is working would be helpful in achieving success and avoiding misunderstandings.
- Knowing that there are alternative ways of working would help partners decide whether they are following the most appropriate approach, and perhaps lead them to experiment with approaches new to them.

Notes

1 The argument presented in this chapter was published as the lead paper in a special issue of the *Contemporary Music Review* on Collaboration in Contemporary Music. See Taylor (2016).
2 For example, see: Savage and Challis (2001), Seddon (2006), Truman (2011), MacDonald & Miell (2000), Gall & Breeze (2008), and Dillon (2004).

References

Adams, John. 2008. *Hallelujah Junction: Composing an American Life*. London: Faber and Faber.
Bennett, Joe. 2012. "Constraint, Collaboration and Creativity in Popular Songwriting Teams." In *The Act of Musical Composition*, edited by Dave Collins, 139–69. Farnham and Burlington VT: Ashgate.

Bentley, Eric. 1981. "Martha Graham's Journey." In *What is Dance? Readings in Theory and Criticism*, edited by Roger Copeland & Marshall Cohen, 197–202. Oxford and New York: Oxford University Press.

Butt, John 2002. *Playing with History: The Historical Approach to Musical Performance*. Cambridge & New York: Cambridge University Press.

Cage, John & Joan Retallack. 1996. *Musicage: Cage Muses on Music*. Middletown CT: Wesleyan University Press, Distributed by University Press of New England.

Clarke, Eric F., Mark Doffman, & Liza Lim. 2013. "Distributed Creativity and Ecological Dynamics: A Case Study of Liza Lim's 'Tongue of the Invisible'." *Music and Letters* 94 (4): 628–63. DOI: 10.1093/ml/gct118

Clarke, Eric F., Mark Doffman, David Gorton, & Stefan Östersjö. 2017. "Fluid Practices, Solid Roles? The Evolution of Forlorn Hope." In *Distributed Creativity: Collaboration and Improvisation in Contemporary Music*, edited by Eric F. Clarke & Mark Doffman, 116–35. Oxford: Oxford University Press. DOI: 10.1093/oso/9780199355914.001.0001

Cunningham, Merce. 1999. *The Dancer and the Dance*. New York and London: Marion Boyars.

Dillenbourg, Pierre. 1999. "Introduction; What Do You Mean by 'Collaborative Learning'?" In *Collaborative Learning: Cognitive and Computational Approaches*, edited by Pierre Dillenbourg, 1–19. Amsterdam: Pergamon.

Dillon, Teresa. 2004. "It's in the Mix Baby: Exploring How Meaning is Created within Music Technology Collaborations." In *Collaborative Creativity: Contemporary Perspectives*, edited by Dorothy Miell & Karen Littleton, 144–57. London: Free Association Books.

Dobson, Elizabeth. 2009. "Serious Misunderstandings: Challenging the Educational and Creative Value of Collaboration for Music Technology Undergraduates." *Forum for Innovation in Music Technology*. Leeds: Leeds College of Music.

Ellis, Samantha. 2017. "The Sister Who Got There First." *The Guardian Review* 1 (7): 16. www.theguardian.com/books/2017/jan/06/anne-bronte-agnes-grey-jane-eyre-charlotte

Etchells, Tim. 1999. *Certain Fragments: Contemporary Performance and Forced Entertainment*. London: Routledge.

Fontaine, Sheryl I. & Susan M. Hunter. 2006. *Collaborative Writing in Composition Studies*. Boston, MA: Thomson Wadsworth.

Fronckowiak, Ann. 2006. *The Oboe Concerto of John Harbison: A Guide to Analysis, Performance, and the Collaboration with the Oboist, William Bennett*. Accessed 08 August 2020. www.semanticscholar.org/paper/The-oboe-concerto-of-John-Harbison%3A-A-guide-to-and-Fronckowiak/083849c33a5e506204bf60278470c0619efe6a19

Gall, Marina & Nick Breeze. 2008. "Music and eJay: An Opportunity for Creative Collaboration in the Classroom." *International Journal of Educational Research* 47 (1): 27–40. DOI: 10.1016/j.ijer.2007.11.008

Gorton, David & Stefan Östersjö. 2016. "Choose Your Own Adventure Music: On the Emergence of Voice in Musical Collaboration." *Contemporary Music Review* 35 (6): 579–98. DOI: 10.1080/07494467.2016.1282596

Hankinson, Ann & Deborah O'Grady. 1981. "In Re: Collaboration." *Perspectives of New Music* 19 (1/2): 200–11.

Hastings, Baird. 1983. *Choreographer and Composer*. Boston MA: Twayne Publishers.

Hayden, Sam & Luke Windsor. 2007. "Collaboration and the Composer: Case Studies from the End of the 20th Century." *Tempo* 61 (2): 28–39. DOI: 10.1017/S0040298207000113

Heisler, Wayne Jnr. 2009. *The Ballet Collaborations of Richard Strauss*. Rochester NY and Woodbridge UK: University of Rochester Press.

Hodgins, Paul. 1992. *Relationships Between Score and Choreography in Twentieth-Century Dance. Music, Movement and Metaphor*. Lewiston and Lampeter: The Edward Mellon Press.

John-Steiner, Vera. 1997. *Notebooks of the Mind: Explorations of Thinking*. Oxford: Oxford University Press.

———. 2000. *Creative Collaboration*. Oxford: Oxford University Press. DOI: 10.1093/acprof:oso/9780195307702.001.0001

Kipnis, Andrew B. 2015 "Agency Between Humanism and Posthumanism: Latour and his Opponents." *Journal of Ethnographic Theory* 5 (2): 43–58. DOI: dx.doi.org/10.14318/hau5.2.004

Lim, Liza. 2020. *Liza Lim, Composer*. Accessed 08 August 2020. lizalimcomposer.com

MacDonald, Raymond & Dorothy Miell. 2000. "Musical Conversations: Collaborating with Friends on Creative Tasks." In *Rethinking Collaborative Learning*, edited by Richard Joiner, Karen Littleton, Dorothy Faulkner & Dorothy Miell, 65–78. London and New York: Free Association Books.

Mercer, Neil. 2000. *Words and Minds: How We Use Language to Work Together*. London and New York: Routledge.

Miell, Dorothy, & Karen Littleton. 2004. *Collaborative Creativity: Contemporary Perspectives*. London: Free Association Books.

Moran, Seana & Vera John-Steiner. 2004. "How Collaboration in Creative Work Impacts Identity and Motivation." In *Collaborative Creativity: Contemporary Perspectives*, edited by Dorothy Miell & Karen Littleton, 11–25. London: Free Association Books.

Robertson, Marta. 1991. "Musical and Choreographic Integration in Copland's and Graham's Appalachian Spring." *The Musical Quarterly* 83 (1): 2–27.

Roche, Heather. 2011. "Dialogue and Collaboration in the Creation of New Works for Clarinet." *Unpublished PhD Thesis*. Huddersfield: University of Huddersfield.

Saunders, Max. 2006. "Secret Agencies. Ford, Conrad, Collaboration and Conspiracy." In *Collaboration in the Arts from the Middle Ages to the Present*, edited by Silvia Bigliazzi, 91–101. Aldershot and Burlington VT: Ashgate.

Savage, Jonathan & Mike Challis. 2001. "Dunwich Revisited: Collaborative Composition and Performance with New Technologies." *British Journal of Music Education* 18 (2: 1): 39–150. DOI: 10.1017/S0265051701000237

Seddon, Frederick A. 2004. "Empathetic Creativity: The Product of Empathetic Attunement." In *Collaborative Creativity: Contemporary Perspectives*, edited by Dorothy Miell & Karen Littleton, 65–78. London: Free Association Books.

———. 2006. "Collaborative Computer-Mediated Music Composition in Cyberspace." *British Journal of Music Education* 273–83. DOI: 10.1017/S0265051706007054

Taylor, Alan. 2016. "Collaboration in Contemporary Music: A Theoretical View." *Contemporary Music Review* 35 (6): 562–78. DOI: 10.1080/07494467.2016.1288316

———. 2018. "An Investigation of the Process of Artistic Creation Provoked by the Attempt to Share It." *Unpublished PhD Thesis, Royal Central School of Speech and Drama.* University of London.

Truman, Sylvia M. 2011. "A Generative Framework for Creativity: Encouraging Creative Collaboration in Children's Music Composition." In *Exploring Children's Creative Narratives*, edited by Dorothy Faulkner & Elizabeth Coates, 212–23. London and New York: Routledge.

Watts, Carol. 2010. "Set, Unset: Collaboration, Encounter and the Scene of Poetry." *Contemporary Music Review* 29 (2): 145–58. DOI: 10.1080/07494467.2010.534921

Watts, Christopher. 2004. "Mixing Things Up: Collaboration, Converging Disciplines, and the Musical Curriculum." *Organised Sound* 9 (3): 295–99. DOI: 10.1017/S1355771804000494

Wishart, Trevor. 1996. *On Sonic Art*. New York & London: Routledge.

Wordsworth, William & Samuel T. Coleridge. 2007. *Lyrical Ballads*. London: Penguin Books.

4 Making musical meanings
The imaginative listener[1]

Introduction

Plato records Socrates, in his defence at his trial, describing how poets '... are like diviners or soothsayers who also say many fine things, but do not understand the meaning of them.' (2016, 25). His words raise the question examined in this chapter. Since composers and performers rely on their subconscious when imagining, they cannot be expected to 'understand' or explain the meaning of their music. Yet music is commonly experienced as meaningful, so how and why does this sense of meaning arise if it cannot be attributed directly to the music makers? To illustrate this point, research by Crispin and Östersjö into the ability of music to communicate specific ideas or emotions led them to conclude that:

> composers and performers might carry out their artistic practice without any overtly emotional intention, yet their compositions and performances may still arouse powerful, though unbidden, emotions in listeners.
>
> (2017, 288)

The implication of their finding is that, even if composers and performers do have a sense that their musical ideas or pieces are meaningful to them, this will not necessarily be the same as any meanings experienced by listeners. As I will show in this chapter, the evidence is also that sensed emotions and meanings provoked in different listeners by the same piece of music are not identical, and so listeners, rather than being recipients of meanings communicated by performers from composers, must have used their individual imaginations to make meanings from musical experiences. As Leech-Wilkinson puts it '... performance triggers the generation of musical meaning in the mind of the listener.' (2012, 1).

One explanation for this, put forward by Cross (2009–10), is that while music and language are both forms of human communication their relationships to the communication of meaning are different. Music, in his view, communicates a sense of 'shared intentionality ... while under-specifying goals.' (2009–10, 179). So, while music may be felt to communicate in related ways to similar people, and to result in senses of shared engagement, its 'meaning' is hard to fix or agree and so it cannot be attributed directly to composers or performers.

However, since music is commonly experienced as communicating meaning or emotions, the question is how this comes about, and why listeners may come to experience more or less specific senses of what a piece of music means to them. The question is quite why listeners experience music as more than just pleasurable 'auditory cheesecake', as Pinker describes it (1997, 534), and why they often use words to describe the meanings they perceive.

It is worth examining the difference, if any, between 'meaning' and 'emotion' in music at this point, since writers on this subject use either term or both. It could be argued, for instance, that a sense of meaning in music could result from experiencing the communication of emotions. The distinction is a pretty fine one though, and in any case, my argument concerns why and how listeners are provoked to sense either of them. However, I do refer to meaning or emotion in two distinct ways, one being the unspecified and perhaps unspecifiable sense of emotion or meaning provoked by a piece of music, and the other the attempted verbalisation of this sense.

I've divided the chapter into two parts. In the first, I examine debates on the source of meaning in art and evidence on the nature of listener perceptions of meaning in music. In the second I examine possible explanations for these perceptions based on studies of music cognition and neurology.

Part 1: The sources of meaning in music

It is important at this stage of the discussion to review the debates which have taken place on whether artists should be treated as the authorities on the meaning of their art. These debates have mainly concerned literary writing rather than music, and the view that a writer's or artist's intentions are key to understanding their art. Cook explains why this idea is not generally accepted in the academic study of music, writing that:

we cannot know what composers *intended* except by means of deduction from what they *did*, and therefore the language of intentions adds nothing to the description of the score.

(Cook 2006, 18)

However, these debates have been too extensive to ignore. In any case, it remains a popular perception that composers speak to us through their music, and so it is worth examining the arguments for and against this view. Also, these debates do offer pointers towards the conclusions I draw later.

Author or authority?

The maker of any art is obviously the author of the art in the narrow sense though, as I showed in Chapter 2, their ideas cannot be said to be just their own. As Fontaine and Hunter put it, the idea that the writer writes alone, and is solely responsible for their work, is a '... romantic representation ...' (2006, xxiii) of the production of art.

The question which has been debated, however, is whether or not the maker of the art should be treated as the author of, or authority on, its meaning. Since this debate has ranged far more widely than music and centred mostly on literature, I will generally refer to artists rather than musicians in this section. There have been two largely separate debates, though they cover much the same ground. The first dates back to Wimsatt and Beardsley's paper *The Intentional Fallacy*, in which they argue that '... the design or intention of the author is neither available nor desirable as a standard for judging the success of a work of literary art ...' (1954, 2).

The first of their arguments is that author's intentions are unavailable because they did not state, or are unable to explain, their art's meanings. They support this with descriptions by poets of how poetry would suddenly occur to them, as verse, rather than being written to communicate meanings, including that by Housman which I quoted in Chapter 2. If ideas just come to artists in this way in the language of their art form, and I quoted many similar examples in Chapter 2, they will be unable to define what their art means beyond a sense personal to themselves. As Beardsley argues in a later paper, we should therefore look to the art, not the artist, in seeking meanings. He quotes the critic Cleanth Brooks who described himself as a poem-reader, not a mind-reader (Beardsley 1992, 33). Brooks aimed to interpret the poems, not to understand the thoughts of the poets.

A study of the creative processes of twenty-five artists lends support to this view that artists should not be looked to in interpreting their art. The artists' descriptions led the authors, Marsh and Vollmer, to conclude that art is '... essentially polyphonic ...' (1991, 114), that is, it is inherently complex and so artists cannot have had definable meanings in mind. Rather, they imagined in ways which led to the making of art in which ambiguity was embedded.

Wimsatt and Beardsley also argue that it would, in any case, be undesirable to base interpretations on statements by artists of their intentions since, if a poem succeeds in communicating as the poet intended, there would be no need to refer to the poet, and if does not succeed there would be no point referring to them (1954, 4).

Much of the debate on what is called 'intentionalism', the view that the intentions of the artist should be central to interpreting art, has focussed on this second issue. I suggest that this is not the main point. If artists do not intend to communicate meanings, and the evidence is certainly that musicians do not in the usual sense of that word, then there would be no point in referring to their alleged intentions in discussing the meaning of their art.

The second debate began with Barthes' essay *Death of the Author*, in which he argues that it is the reader who makes the meanings. He writes that:

> a text is made of multiple writings, drawn from many cultures and entering into mutual relations in dialogue, parody, contestation, but there is one place where this multiplicity is focused, and that place is the reader, not, as was hitherto said, the author.
>
> (Barthes 1977, 148)

His argument is the same as the one I put forward in Chapter 2, that ideas arise from a dialogue provoked by a wide variety of influences and stimuli. Due to the art's resulting complexity, meanings will necessarily be made by each individual reader so it would be wrong to look to the author in interpreting the art. Derrida argues in a similar vein that texts must simply be taken as they are without reference to the author since the text or other art is unable to explain itself. He describes how:

> Wandering the streets he [the text] doesn't even know who he is, ...
> He repeats the same thing every time he is questioned on the street corner, but he can no longer repeat his origin.
>
> (1976, 143–4)

Opposition and qualifications

Two counter-arguments are that:

1. The creation of art is an intentional act and so we cannot dismiss the author's intentions as irrelevant.
2. Interpretations of art will be made, and so there must be some standard for judging them.

Gaut and Livingston make the first argument, writing that it is important to construct '… the artwork as the product of the artist's actions.' (2003, 1). The second argument is put forward by Hirsch, who considers that there must be a correct meaning to a text, since '… if the meaning of a text is not the author's, then no interpretation can possibly correspond to *the* meaning of the text …'. (1992, 14).

These statements should be read in light of the general agreement that art is experienced as complex and ambiguous. This is accepted by the proponents of intentionalism, for instance by Hirsch, who writes that 'Ambiguity is not the same as indeterminateness.' (Hirsch 1992, 21). The problem with this, if the aim is to agree whether an interpretation corresponds with the artist's intentions, is how to define what is communicated by an inherently ambiguous piece of art in order to establish whether this fits with their claimed intentions.

While artists intend to make their art and to give it a character with which they are satisfied, it does not follow that they intend to communicate meanings which can be defined in a way which makes possible agreement on their 'correctness' or otherwise. Statements that art has a '… real …' (Hirsch 1992, 15) meaning or, as Gaut and Livingston put it, that art can be interpreted '… correctly …' (2003, 6), appear to rest on the assumption that artists intend to communicate definable meanings.

However, the evidence is that artists aim to offer experiences in the language of their art rather than to communicate definable meanings. An experience will, by definition, be felt separately by each person. As the leading post-war writer on hermeneutics (the theory and method of interpretation), Gadamer, writes '… understanding includes a reflective dimension from the very beginning.' (1997, 45). That is, understanding arises from reflection on experience rather than simply from receiving information. One person's understanding may therefore differ from another's. The result for music, as Delis, Fleer, and Kerr point out, is that '… there is no guarantee that one person's designated interpretation of a musical passage will be like another's.' (1978, 215).

Other writers have put forward arguments on a spectrum between those I've quoted so far. For instance, commenting on Barthes' view, Foucault (1979) argues that the role of the author cannot be wholly dismissed, since '… an author's name is not simply an element in a discourse … Such a name permits one to group together a certain number of texts, define them, differentiate them from and contrast them to others.' (1979, 5). We therefore experience the art of any one artist in a way affected by our perception of that artist. However, Foucault questions the idea of the author as an individual whose intended meanings are the essence of the art. He considers that we should '… no longer hear the questions that have been rehashed for so long: Who really spoke? … And what part of his deepest self did he express in his discourse?' (Foucault 1979, 14).

Burke (2008) takes this argument further in his detailed critique of Barthes, Foucault, and Derrida. Burke considers that Barthes sees 'The death of the author is the first and sufficient step towards refusing to assign a "secret", or ultimate meaning, to the text …' (2008, 23). Burke argues that it is not necessary to abandon the concept of the author to make this break between the idea of authorship of art and the authorship of meanings made from art, since the relationship between artists and their art can be seen in other ways. For instance, he notes that many writers perceive their writing as if it were by a person other than themselves, the 'writer' (2008, 50). As Harkaway puts it, 'Writing is always some kind of encounter with another person that lives in your head …' (2017, 11). If an artist does not feel they are the person responsible for their art, then they do not need to be dethroned from their position of author-god in the way Barthes claims.

This is the crux of my argument. The question should not be what artists may or may not intend to communicate, but how meanings are made from art. For music, as I will show later, the answer appears to be that meanings are made through listening, and so are personal to each listener. Listeners, of course, include composers and performers as they make music.

In this context, some writers argue that authors do define the form or character of their art, even if they may not define the meanings made from it. Levinson distinguishes the categorical, as opposed to the semantic, intentions of artists. By categorical, he means intentions '… that govern not what a work is to mean but how it is to be conceived, approached, classified on a fundamental level.' (Levinson 1992, 222). A composer can intend to write a concerto (a category of art), but that does not imply that they define the meaning (semantic content) of the concerto. However, to present the concerto as something else would clearly be contrary to the composer's intentions.

Artists also, Livingston argues, need the intention to create art of a certain character to guide their work. Writing about composers, he says that:

> once a musician is settled on the plan of composing a musical work, this intention initiates thinking about how to bring this about, and when the time comes, helps bring closure to these compositional efforts.
>
> (Livingston 2005, 15)

In other words, composers need to have intentions concerning the character of their music to be able to judge its progress. Any such intentions will, of course, be bound up with the nature of the project in which they are engaged. The process of imagining musical ideas does not take place in a vacuum but is deeply affected by the other people and instruments involved, and the intended means (notation or otherwise) of communication which the composer chooses.

While this is clearly the case, a composer's thinking will begin with the imagination of musical ideas rather than with intentions which are then translated into music. They are likely to judge these ideas according to whether they please them and feel right in the context of the project and people and instruments involved, rather than against any preconceived intentions concerning the piece they are writing. There is no need to have the intention to write music of a character imagined at or near the start to be able to compose effectively.

I remain unconvinced by the argument that artists' intentions are central to understanding art, not least because it does not fit with the view of the musical imagination proposed in Chapter 2. Three aspects of the imaginative process in composition are relevant here, and together they suggest that composers should not be treated as authorities on the meaning of the music they write. These are that:

1. Composers imagine in music. Since the process consists of thinking in music and in terms of instruments and means of notation, verbal descriptions of the music's meaning, whether by the composer or anyone else, will not communicate the full sense of the music. Too much will be lost in translation for such verbal descriptions to be capable of representing the composer's intentions.
2. Musical ideas appear from subconscious thought, so composers will be unable to describe anything beyond a meaning personal to

them. Any sense of meaning they do experience will result from their actual or imagined listening, and so other listeners may hear different meanings in the music.
3. Composers' ideas arise from a dialogue between influences, and so the music they write will have complexity embedded within it. As a result, listeners will not all hear the same things in the music or imagine the same meanings.

As Levinson and Livingston point out, artists do have intentions concerning the form (category) and, probably, the character of the art they are creating, even if they realise the latter as they work on a piece. But it does not follow from this that artists intend to communicate meanings in the sense of interpretations which can be agreed. Composers certainly aim to create experiences, but there can be no guarantee that listeners will hear a piece of music in the same way as one another or as may have been imagined by the composer. This is because both the sense that the music is meaningful and any more exact view of what it means arise from the listening experience. Any claim that a listener has heard the music correctly will as a result, and by definition, be unverifiable. This is evidenced by studies of the listening process.

Listener meaning making

Studies of the perception (reception of information) and cognition (processing of information, for instance by defining meanings) of music show that listeners experience senses of emotion and meaning in music rather than simply finding it pleasurable. For example, in his study of the strong experiences of music recalled by nearly 1000 people, Gabrielsson found that many described these experiences in verbal and quite specific terms. For instance, one fairly common experience was of being provoked to feel '... religious.' (2011, 390–1). His research shows that many people experience intense emotional communication through music, but also that they often describe the meaning which they feel is communicated by the music. The perceptive part of the process consists of the intense response, and the cognitive part of the attempt to define this, a process which Gabrielsson sees as resulting from the comparison of perceptions with previous experience (2011, 382).

However, the evidence is that music does not provoke the same response, strong or otherwise, in listeners consistently. Rather, as Gabrielsson puts it 'Different individuals react differently, and reactions to the same music may vary on different occasions.' (2011a, 547). Some, at least, of these reactions must differ from those of the musicians who produced the music, and so it cannot be said that music has a stable meaning intended by the composer, or even that a specific performer's interpretation has a stable meaning.

For example, Downey showed that, when listeners are asked to write their impressions of pieces of music, they may record similar general reactions but their detailed accounts of the same piece differ (1897, 63). She found that the '... formal content [meaning] seems to be furnished entirely by the mood, associations or temperament of the individual [listener].' (1897, 69). A similar conclusion follows from Nattiez' experiment with *L'Apprenti Sorcier* by Dukas, which was played to 300 schoolchildren who did not know the piece and were not told the story or title. They were asked 'This music tells a story. What is it?' (1990, 246). They invented a wide range of contrasting stories, none of which were about sorcerers or their apprentices (1990, 244). If Dukas intended to tell the original story through his piece, Nattiez' study shows that the music itself does not achieve this. The children's experiences of the music led them to invent contrasting stories, and these meanings were made by the children and not by the composer.

My study of audience understandings of two of my own pieces points to the same conclusion (2020, See Section 3). While the audiences described a variety of senses of meaning which I can see connect with the general characters of the pieces as I had imagined them, their more detailed responses shared two characteristics:

- They were far more elaborate than anything verbally expressible which I had imagined. I had thought in music and general affects, while the listeners often described detailed understandings.
- The audience members described contrasting understandings of the pieces, which suggests that they made meanings individually from their experience of the music, rather than by de-coding meanings communicated by the music.

This phenomenon, of listeners hearing different meanings in the same piece, is illustrated by a disagreement on the interpretations of the *Andante con moto* from Beethoven's *Piano Concerto No.4 in G major, Op. 58*. Jander argues that the movement is programmatic and related to an episode from the Orpheus legend (1985, 196) and cannot be fully accounted for by structural or harmonic analysis (1985, 205). Cone disputes this and presents a structural analysis of the movement independent of narrative interpretations, though he accepts that the movement could be read as an enactment of a different part of the legend (1985, 285). Kerman questions whether the interpretation in terms of the Orpheus legend can be fully maintained but considers that there is nothing capricious about it (1992, 90). Jander argues for his original view in a subsequent paper, showing that Beethoven stated literary sources for pieces several times (1995, 32) and lived at a time when aestheticians had urged composers to draw on real or fictional people to bring expression into instrumental music (1995, 32). All three writers accept that Beethoven's intentions remain unknown.

A model of this process of the perception of meaning from music presented by Crispin and Östersjö (2017) helps explain why listeners develop contrasting understandings. They describe the process as one of inferring meaning, inference being necessary to make meanings from music because it is characterised by what Cross calls '... semantic indeterminacy ...' (2009–10, 192), that is, the precise meaning is not definable. Crispin and Östersjö's view is that expression is inferred in composers by performers, and in performers by audiences (2017, 301), and so the experience of emotion or meaning in music results from these imaginative inferences.

A detailed study of listening by Clarke (2005), based on a wide range of examples, lends support to this view that meanings are made through listening and are made separately by each listener. He examines the way in which listeners '... seek out and respond to ...' (2005, 41) stimuli which provoke a sense of meaning. He describes listening as 'ecological' since the process is always one of responding to a specific piece of music, which '... does not proceed independently of the affordances of musical materials ...' (Clarke 2005, 43). The process is two-way and results from the interaction between listeners' perceptions and the character of each specific piece.

Music cognition, in Clarke's view, is therefore an individual process, but people who '... share a common environment, and experience common perceptual learning or adaptation.' (2005, 191) are likely to respond in similar ways to the same performance. The evidence from the studies I quoted above is, however, that detailed understandings will vary, even between culturally similar listeners.

It is also the case that people from different backgrounds are likely to listen to music in contrasting ways. Becker, writing as an ethnomusicologist, argues that:

> Emotions relating to music are culturally embedded and socially constructed, and can usefully be viewed as being about an individual within a community, rather than being exclusively about internal states.
>
> (2011, 145)

Becker gives a series of examples from different cultures to illustrate the many forms of listening and the expectations and understandings of music in those cultures. She uses the term 'habitus of listening' for culturally-based forms of listening and responding to music and emphasises that the stereotype of the silent middle-class listener in the concert hall is itself a culturally-specific habitus of listening (2011, 134–44). She considers that within any one culture there will be a shared way of listening to music which is neither wholly static nor fluid (Becker 2004, 86) and which will vary to an extent between individuals (2004, 69). Music, then, is heard differently by people in different cultures, and detailed responses to a piece of music vary even within one culture.

It might be objected to the argument I am developing that, though verbal statements of the meanings of music will vary, music may nevertheless communicate in a detailed way in purely musical terms. Mendelssohn seemed to express this sense in writing that:

> People often complain that music is ambiguous, that their ideas on the subject always seem so vague, whereas everyone understands words; with me it is exactly the reverse; not merely with regard to entire sentences, but also as to individual words; these, too, seem to me so ambiguous, so vague, so unintelligible when compared with genuine music, which fills the soul with a thousand things better than words.
>
> (Mendelssohn Bartholdy 2001, 276)

This is close to the view proposed by Tagg (2013), who argues that music communicates more or less precise, though not verbally definable, meanings. He gives examples to support his view that sounds constitute a '... meaningful system of sonic representation.' (Tagg 2013, 5), and that music can communicate fairly specific meanings in the appropriate social context. Like Clarke, he notes that '... different individuals within the same culture tend repeatedly to respond to the same music in quite similar ways ...' (Tagg 2013, 170).

However, there is a gap in his argument that music communicates fairly precise meanings. While I think any dedicated musician or listener would have felt the same experience of detailed communication as Mendelssohn, the problem with Tagg's argument is that, in order to establish that a piece of music communicates fairly precise meanings, it would be necessary to define what it communicates, and to do so in words to make agreement possible. These 'translations' would vary from one listener to another, and so we would be no closer to the precise meaning of the music. Definitive agreement on the nature of such an experience is, by definition, impossible. The sense of a detailed and complex experience felt by a composer, performer or listener is not of the same nature as the communication of more or less precise meanings.

I have seen no convincing evidence to support the view that musical meanings result from listeners understanding meanings which composers and performers intend to communicate. My own study is the only one I am aware of in which composer 'intentions', insofar as they could be defined, and listener perceptions were compared (Taylor 2020). The findings do not support the view that meanings intended by the composer, or capable of being agreed, are communicated through music. Only the general profile of the listener responses corresponded with my own thoughts to the extent that I was aware of them, and the detailed listener understandings were quite new to me.

The evidence from these studies does not support the idea of intentionalism, but suggests instead that:

- Meanings are made as an imaginative response to the listening experience rather than being communicated by music. These meanings may consist of both a holistic sense that the music is meaningful and a more detailed understanding of its meaning.
- While socially similar listeners are likely to have overlapping holistic perceptions of a performance, these will not be identical, and their detailed understandings are often contrasting. Socially or culturally different listeners may hear the same music in contrasting ways.

The problem, then, remains. Music is clearly a form of communication, listeners commonly feel that it communicates emotions or meanings, yet their responses to the same piece often diverge. While the studies quoted in this section reflect these patterns of cognition, they do not explain them. This is the subject of Part 2.

Part 2: How the sense of musical meaning may arise

Music perception and cognition

There is, as DeNora puts it, '... a pervasive idea in Western culture that music possesses social and emotional content ...' (2000, 21), in other words, that it contains meanings. There is clearly a difference between the idea that music itself contains content or meanings and the view that the sense of meaning results from experiencing music, and this is central to my argument in this chapter. If music contains emotional content, then that content must have been intended in some way by those involved in creating it, and much of the focus of study of musical meaning should be on how the music makers achieve this. If, on the other hand, musical 'content' is the result of music's capacity to provoke a sense of meaning in the listener, then the focus should be mainly on the processes of music perception and cognition.

Evidence which supports the latter view is presented by Jackendoff and Lerdahl (2006) in their investigation of emotional communication through music. They conclude that music enables listeners to construct their own senses of emotion and drama from the listening experience rather than that the music itself contains emotions. As Crispin and Östersjö put it, while the formation of musical expression depends on an '... equal and engaged relationship between composers, performers and audience ...' nevertheless '... all musical listening is ... a way to launch creative imagination in an individual.' (2017, 301–2).

The question I investigate in the rest of this chapter is quite how music comes to be perceived as meaningful by listeners. I mentioned two different kinds of meaning in the previous section, and the distinction between them is central to this discussion. Meaning can be experiential, as when music is felt to be meaningful with no further explanation required. Alternatively, one thing may designate, represent, or 'mean' another. If music communicates designated meanings directly, and I don't think it does in all but a few cases, then we might be able to agree what they are. However, since the sense of musical meaning seems to be largely experiential, it is by definition made by the person who has the experience, and it would be inaccurate to say that the musicians or the music communicate the meanings. The question is why such experiential meanings are felt.

A longstanding explanation of experiential meaning in music, proposed by Langer (1942), is that music can reflect the shape of emotions without representing or communicating them directly. Her view has been described as being that '... music acquires meaning through its natural resemblance to the dynamic forms of emotional life.' (Thompson 2015, 180). Davies agrees with this, contrasting the idea of a '... resemblance between music and the realm of human emotion.' (2006, 181) with the view that music '... presents a narrative or drama about a persona who experiences ...' (2006, 188). He criticises the latter view, writing:

> For myself, the experience is one of hearing the music as possessing the appearances of emotion, while regarding it as neither alive nor haunted by a persona.
>
> (2006, 191)

Langer's book was written before modern developments in the understanding of human thinking, and some later writers such as Budd question her view. He points to the ability of music to seem analogous to feelings (Budd 1985, 113) and contrasts this with Langer's view of music as consisting of unconsummated symbols (it seems to stand for things but we are unable to say what). However, Budd's argument differs from Langer's mainly because it is based on a modern understanding of the importance of analogy in human thinking. After all, analogies are perceived between things which have a resemblance but do not represent one another. This is close to Langer's concept of the unconsummated symbol, which seems to represent something, but we cannot define quite what. Whichever way the view is expressed, the point is that it is the similarities between music and human experience which lead us to experience music as meaningful.

In her review of the role of analogy in listening, concerned primarily with the recognition of style and gesture in music rather than the making of meanings, Deliège (2006) concludes by referring to the importance of the application of a listener's previous knowledge of styles and gestures as they seek to follow music. She quotes Lerdahl and Jackendoff's conclusion in their earlier study that '... the listener brings to his hearing – a knowledge that enables him to organise and make coherent the surface patterns of pitch, attack, duration, intensity, timbre, and so forth.' (1983, 3). Deliège's argument from this is that listeners perceive music as making sense, in stylistic terms at least, through comparison with their previous knowledge in the search for analogies.

Communication by analogy is identified by several writers as the means by which listeners perceive emotions or meaning in music. Zbikowski, for example, considers that music can provide '... sonic analogues for various dynamic processes that are common in human experience.' (2017, 190). Analogy is also proposed as a reason for story-perception in music. Maus suggests that there exist '... analogies between instrumental music and discourses normally understood as narrative.' (2005, 466) and prefers this view to the idea that music may represent a narrative. Similarly, Toolan describes music as an analogy for a system of symbols which have meanings (2011, para 15) and suggests that this is why it can be experienced as if it were a narrative. The implication is that the sense that music is meaningful results from perceiving analogies for experiences we know or can imagine, rather than by communicating meanings directly.

It is argued that the perception of analogies for emotions or meanings in music results from our embodied engagement as we listen. In this context, the term 'embodied' includes every bodily response to music from physical engagement through to sensory experiencing. For example, a team led by Juslin (2011) examined a series on ways in which emotion may be experienced through music and describe a process which they call 'emotional contagion' through which '… an emotion is induced by a piece of music because the listener perceives the emotional expression of the music and the 'mimics' this expression internally.' (2011, 622). It is the listener's engagement in, and mimicking of, the music which leads them to feel emotions and, therefore, a sense that the music constitutes a meaningful communication.

The term 'embodied music cognition' is used by Leman (2008) for the way in which music is experienced throughout our bodies, not just interpreted in our minds. As I mentioned in Chapter 2, Damasio (2006) both challenges the idea that the mind operates independently of the body, and demonstrates the necessity for intact neural connections integrating brain and bodily responses in order to enable the patients he studied to experience fully developed feelings and to make judgements and choices. This integrated mind–body process is the mechanism of embodied music cognition, which Leman describes as:

> an action-based account of subjective involvement with music. In this approach, direct involvement with music is assumed to be based on physical energies having an impact on the human body and mind.
>
> (2008, 28)

A similar view is proposed by Cox, who sees our engagement in music as active rather than passive since we mentally or physically imitate the music (Cox 2011). He also comments on the way we sub-vocalise as we listen, imitating the music as if we were singing (Cox 2001, 196). He considers that this mimetic bodily engagement in music leads us to experience it as meaningful. Music, then, will be experienced as meaningful because it provokes us to engage with it rather than because it contains meanings.

Since music cognition appears to depend on an integrated brain–body response, this may explain why it is felt to be meaningful by analogy with previous experience. The result of embodied engagement in music is likely to be that we feel it to be in some way meaningful since we would not engage with something which left us cold and so seemed devoid of meaning. The detailed nature of this engagement will lead us to perceive similarities between music and previous experiences which provoked related senses of engagement, and so as analogous to those experiences. We may also, of course, perceive analogies with experiences we can imagine.

The evidence is that perception through analogy is fundamental to human thinking in general, and numerous studies have shown that we try to understand experiences by seeking analogies in our accumulated understandings. For instance, Novick shows from her experiments on how people deal with new situations that they are better able to explain these if they can see them as analogous to something they already know (1988, 51). This view is supported by several of the contributors to the collection edited by Vosniadou and Ortony (1989), including Gentner who describes the way we compare new information with existing knowledge in order to understand the former (1989, 200–6). In a separate study, Deliège considers that analogical thinking of this type is the basis of artistic communication, describing our use of '... perceptual mechanisms to react by analogous strategies ...' (2006, 74) to musical experiences, and noting the implication of this that each listener will follow a unique process in doing so (2006, 74).

There remains the question of exactly how this process operates in the brain, which I examine in the next section, but the first conclusion to be drawn from the studies quoted is that listeners perceive meaning in music because they engage with it and so feel it to be analogous to human experience.

The second conclusion is that music is experienced complete, rather than being an aggregate of meanings, and so any statement of its meaning can be only in a partial version of the experience. Nevertheless, listeners do commonly attempt to define the meaning of musical experiences. This sense of music as a holistic experience is described by Schütz, who writes that music can only be re-experienced by '... re-immersing oneself in the ongoing flux ...' and that '... it will "take as much time" to reconstitute the work in recollection as to experience it for the first time.' (Schütz 1951, 91). Merleau-Ponty makes the same point, writing that:

> Once the performance has come to an end, we cannot do anything in our intellectual analyses of the music but refer back to the moment of the experience.
>
> (2014, 188)

If it is accepted that the experience of music is unsummarisable, then music cannot be said to communicate definable meanings because any meaning stated will be less complete than the experience of the music. Even so, listeners do commonly describe their own, often detailed, sense of a designated meaning in music, as shown by several of the studies quoted in the previous section. These studies also show that, while listeners from similar backgrounds may perceive the same performances in related ways, they still tend to describe contrasting detailed meanings. Each of these different meanings must inevitably be narrower than the complete musical experience.

The two aspects of music cognition which I suggest stand out from these studies are the perception of music as analogous to human experience, and the sense of music as an unsummarisable, holistic experience but one which we may still try to define. However, these are observations of effects rather than explanations of why and how music can provoke these senses. To say that music communicates by analogy, or that we experience it holistically but try to define its meaning, is to leave unanswered the question of how we come to perceive music in these ways.

Possible explanations can be found in aspects of the neurological processes which operate in response to music. Analogy and embodied sensory perception have been linked to the operation of mirror neurons, though the directness of this link has been questioned. The tendency to perceive in a complex and holistic way and yet to define narrower designated meanings can be linked to the contrasting modes of operation of the two brain hemispheres. It would, however, be a mistake, as Juslin (2019) explains, to attribute experiences of music to purely neurological processes. He examines a series of brain mechanisms which are engaged as we experience music, but points out that a psychological theory is needed to explain why emotions are experienced as these brain areas respond to music (2019, 253).

Juslin refers to Gibson's concept of 'affordances', which the latter applies primarily to visual perception (Gibson 1986). Gibson's argument is that vision does not consist of a series of snapshots, but of a constant flow which the viewer participates in shaping. As an old-fashioned guidebook might have put it, 'The hill affords a delightful prospect of the city and the bay beyond.' The view from the hill offers this possibility, but the viewer chooses how to see and experience it. Similarly, music affords the listener the possibility of the communication of emotions, and this does not happen automatically through a neurological process but depends on the psychological response of the listener. My argument in the next section is, therefore, that there are brain mechanisms which <u>enable</u> and <u>lead</u> listeners to sense music as analogous to human experience or to verbalise our understandings, rather than that these mechanisms <u>cause</u> them to respond in these ways.

Embodied cognition and analogies. Mirrors in the mind?

Embodied music cognition and analogy perception can be related to the form of human cognition known as action understanding – we observe or imitate an action and so feel that we understand it. This concept is reflected in Godøy's description of the tendency to perceive and understand music through '... incessant mental simulation of action ...' (2010, 122) and in Leman's view that embodied perception consists of 'the mirroring of action and perception' (2010, 148). The latter uses the term 'gesture' for all aspects of music which appear to move and explains that:

> through gesture, music can be experienced as the action of a dynamic organism similar to a human organism. Such an experience allows for the construction of meaningful relationships with the structural properties of music (pitch, rhythm, articulation, timbre) as well as with its cultural/historical contexts.
>
> (2010, 126)

If we feel we understand music due to our active engagement in simulating what we hear, then it will seem to us that it has meaning, and we may perceive such meanings as analogous to human experiences. This suggests that, in the case of music, action understanding and the perception of analogies are linked. Both have been connected to mirroring systems in the brain through which distinct phenomena are said to be perceived as similar.

Mirror neurons were discovered in the brains of monkeys in the 1990s and were subsequently claimed to exist in humans. A team led by Gallese, including several of those involved in their discovery, describe these neurons as the basis of 'action recognition' (1996, 593). An overlapping team of neuroscientists led by Umilta later found that a similar pattern of neuron firing occurred when part of an action was concealed. The authors argue that this may demonstrate that the monkey understood the action even though they could not see all of it, and so '... that the mirror neurons' matching mechanism could underpin action understanding.' (2001, 161). The claim is that the firing of the same neurons when an action is performed, observed, or observed but partly hidden, shows that these neurons are the means by which actions are both recognised and understood, and so that this limited number of neurons in the motor areas of the brain are the mechanism behind action understanding. As a team led by Rizzolatti argue '... we understand an [observed] action because the motor representation of that action is activated in our brain.' (2001, 661). This seems questionable, at least on the grounds that the neuronal firing might indicate the ability to mentally simulate an action without it necessarily being understood. However, if this finding is valid, it suggests that this mechanism may underly the way our embodied engagement in music can lead to a sense of understanding and meaning.

This is the essence of the wider claim arising from this research, that mirror neurons are the means by which related stimuli are perceived as analogous to one another. This link is made by Gallese and Goldman, who argue that the process observed by these research teams, of the same neurons firing in reaction to parallel experiences, enables us to perceive similarities (1998). As Gallese points out in a later paper, human mirror neurons may have evolved for sensory-motor functions and only later come to be used for social cognition (2008, 163). He considers that these neurons are the basis of the human capacity to understand others' intentional behaviour, and, therefore, that the brain activities involved in achieving this understanding are rooted in our sensory and bodily functioning (2009, 536).

The implication of these research claims for music perception is that action understanding leads to the sense that we understand the music because we perceive it as analogous to human experience. A team led by Molnar-Szakacs describe how:

> Without any reliance on language, an individual can express their emotional state through sound, and another individual can immediately comprehend and interpret this sound signal, based on their own motor, emotional, and musical experiences.
>
> (2012, 324)

These claims, and claims on this subject by many other research teams, are challenged by Hickok in a detailed review of the field. He argues that there are alternative explanations for the experimental observations and that, for instance, the firing of the mirror neurons concerned when an action is partly hidden does not prove that the action is understood through these neurons (2009, 1233). On the question of mirror neurons and action understanding, Hickok writes that:

> the proposal has never been adequately tested in monkeys, and in humans there is strong empirical evidence, in the form of physiological and neuropsychological (double-) dissociations, against the claim.
>
> (2009, 1229)

Hickok's challenge, and those made by other writers such as Lingnau (2009) and Churchland (2011), is to the view that action understanding relies just on the operation of mirror neurons, not to the concept itself. In a later and more comprehensive study Hickok reviews a wide range of neurological research from which he proposes an alternative explanation of action understanding not reliant solely on mirror neurons. In reviewing research on embodied cognition in humans, he shows that '... the motor system fails to capture the semantics of actions.' (2014, 159). That is, the operation of sensory and motor systems in the brain do not by themselves lead to understanding or a sense of meaning. He quotes research by a team led by Binder who carried out a meta-analysis of 120 studies in which the brain areas active in conceptual and semantic processing were tracked (2009). These areas were found to be wholly separate from the brain areas involved in the sensory and motor systems, which include the mirror neurons. The implication is that motor/sensory systems do not by themselves lead to understanding or a sense of meaning.

Hickok's proposal is that action understanding requires the involvement of both the sensory/motor and the largely separate conceptual/semantic areas of the brain. When we receive sensory input, whether through physical movement or any other sense, this stimulus is first registered in the motor/sensory areas of the brain. However, as Hickok explains, understanding of this stimulus requires the involvement of the conceptual/semantic brain areas. This is because understanding new stimuli requires their interpretation in terms of our (constantly updated) existing knowledge.

The key element of Hickok's proposal, that meanings are made through the comparison of new stimuli with existing knowledge, is close to the conclusions drawn in a number of studies of music. As Hargreaves, Hargreaves, and North put it '... new sensory input is interpreted in the light of the perceiver's accumulated schemata, or mental representations ...' (2012, 160), describing these as mediating all musical activities, including listening (2012, 169). Reybrouck puts forward the same view, writing that dealing with music '... entails a constructive process of sense-making that matches the perceptual input against a knowledge base ...' (2006, 45).

The concept of a pre-existing schemata or knowledge base within which we perceive is close to Bakhtin's concept of the heteroglossia (1981, 263) which gives rise to, and is reflected in, the complexity of novels, and also to Barthes '... immense dictionary ...' from which a writer draws their ideas (1977, 147). Every person has their own complex set of accumulated experiences and understandings, and this forms the background to, and source of, our imagining whether making or listening to music. It is the reason why people from related social backgrounds, who may have similar understandings, are likely to perceive music in ways related to one another, whereas people from different cultures may listen to music in contrasting ways.

In light of this, the process of the embodied perception of music leading to a sense of analogy for human experience could be described as follows:

- We hear music, and the motor/sensory areas of the brain register acoustic and movement stimuli due to our embodied engagement.
- The semantic/cognitive areas of the brain become engaged as we seek to make sense of these stimuli.
- Any sense of understanding of the musical stimuli will arise from the listener's accumulated experience, and so the music may be perceived as analogous to that experience or experiences the listener is able to imagine.

This seems a more complete explanation of music perception through embodied engagement and analogy than the idea that such perception relies solely on limited areas of the motor/sensory parts of the brain, the mirror neurons, or wider mirroring systems. In particular, the view that understandings emerge from a comparison between new musical stimuli and our memory of previous experiences can explain why music may be perceived as analogous to human experience.

The implication is that the process of embodied perception of musical meanings through analogy is likely to be, to a fair extent, involuntary. If we do perceive and seek to understand in the way described, any perception that music is analogous to human experience will lead us on to feel that it is meaningful.

Music of the hemispheres

The other question I posed at the start of this section concerned why listeners often try to verbalise and define this sense of experiential communication through music. Examples of this tendency include the many studies in which the authors attempt to define the narrative content of pieces of instrumental music, largely pieces from the Nineteenth Century.[2] My argument is that music of that era is often perceived as analogous to a story, and this may provoke listeners to explain such perceived stories to themselves verbally and in designated terms.

The general nature of this effect has long been observed, for instance by the Roman poet Horace who described two stages of human perception. He wrote:

> For nature has so formed us that we feel inwardly any changes in our fortunes ... it is only afterwards that she expresses these feelings in us by means of the tongue.
>
> (Horace 2000, 101)

His description anticipated findings by modern neurologists on the way experiences are felt and subsequently articulated verbally, and the evidence of a connection between this and the contrasting functioning of the two hemispheres of the brain.

The study of brain hemispheres has, it is important to note, been bedevilled by myths and disproven theories. In a book on myths in popular psychology, the authors Lilienfeld, Lynn, Ruscio, and Beyerstein show that what they call Myth #2, the idea that some people are left-brained and others right-brained, is just that – a myth (2010, 25–8). However, there is clear evidence of differences between the modes of operation of the two hemispheres, and it is this contrast which is relevant here rather than differences between the functions they carry out.

There is certainly some evidence of hemispheric specialisms in relation to music and speech. Zatorre and Belin (2001) tested people's responses to varying sound pitches and found that the left hemisphere is superior in handling more rapidly changing sounds whereas the right is better at responding to a wider range of pitches. They relate this to the greater reliance on the left hemisphere in processing speech, which requires dealing with more rapid changes in emphasis. Music requires a greater ability to respond to pitch variations, and so there is a bias in processing towards the right hemisphere (2001, 950). A recent study by a team led by Albouy found, similarly, that when people listen to songs '... the neural decoding of speech and melodies depends on activity patterns in left and right auditory regions, respectively.' (2020, 1043).

Two leaders in the field of music psychology conclude, however, that there is only limited evidence that the processing of music relies on parts of one or other brain hemisphere. In his comprehensive study, Patel concludes that '... hemispheric asymmetries for speech and music perception certainly exist, but are more subtle than generally appreciated.' (2008, 75–6). Thompson, similarly, concludes that there are no simple associations of this type (2015, 139).

However, there is evidence of contrasts between the forms of perception dominant in the two brain hemispheres, rather than the functions they carry out, and these can be related to the tendency of listeners to construct explanations for musical experiences. One of the leading experts in the field, Gazzaniga, summarises many studies of the functioning of the hemispheres (1998), including an experiment in which images were shown just to the left eye, controlled by the right hemisphere, or just to the right eye (left hemisphere). The people in the study were asked to explain the images, and they interpreted those shown only to the right hemisphere in terms of the relationships they had perceived between images shown only to the left. His conclusion is that '... the left hemisphere seeks explanations for why events occur ...' (1998, 55), including explanations for images shown only to the left eye/right hemisphere, whereas experiences are perceived in a more literal way in the right hemisphere (1998, 55).

Gazzaniga contributed to work led by Metcalfe, which showed that the right hemisphere is superior in terms of accuracy of memory while the left tends to generalise by encoding interpretations as well as actual memories (1995). He also took part in a study led by Wolford which found that, due to the operation of the left hemisphere, people try to make sense of experiences and seek patterns in information even when there are none (2000).

The same distinction is drawn by several writers on music. Bever and Chiarello found that '... the left hemisphere is dominant for analytical processing and the right for holistic processing.' (1974, 94), a finding replicated by Lotze, Sheler, and Birbaumer (2006, 276). Brattico and Tervaniemi (2006, 303) also list numerous studies in which this difference was found.

A development of this view, that experiences are registered holistically in the right hemisphere and the left seeks to explain them, is proposed by McGilchrist (2009), and he supports it with a wealth of evidence. He takes the argument a step further in arguing that left-hemisphere processing reduces the right-hemisphere experience to a less complete form and that the process is sequential. For music, which he refers to frequently, his view would be that the musical experience is initially registered holistically mainly in the right hemisphere, and that the left then seeks to narrow this down in order to define it. Parts of his argument, in which he goes beyond the neurological evidence and proposes an essentially moral view of the superiority of right-hemisphere perception, have been challenged.[3]

This contrast between the forms of perception in the two hemispheres could explain why people may try to summarise their musical experiences in words. Music perceived initially and holistically mainly on the right hemisphere may be felt to be analogous to human experiences. The left hemisphere may then try to interpret this sense of analogy. Words may be used, as they must be if this interpretation is to be described, even to oneself, and the left hemisphere bias towards processing language may lead us to do so.

This could explain the contrast found in a study led by Juslin between two types of emotional response to music, one of which the researchers describe as episodic and the other as semantic (2011, 609). The episodic response is immediate yet fades. The semantic response relates to a judgement of the emotional effect made after the event, and the team of researchers note that this type of subsequent judgement may be inaccurate. This is the same distinction as that made by McGilchrist between a right-hemisphere-based holistic perception followed by a left-hemisphere-based process of narrowing down the experience in the attempt to understand it. This narrowed down, or semantic, response will be inaccurate simply because it is less complete.

Again, this process will to some extent be involuntary. The distinct ways in which the brain hemispheres operate may lead us, whether we wish it or not, to seek to translate the experiential meanings of music into semantic interpretations to explain them to ourselves or others. Listeners can, and often do, retain the holistic impression of music rather than pinning down and explaining the experience, but they are likely to find some difficulty in doing so.

A view of meaning making from music

The evidence is that listeners, far from being a passive recipient of a composer's 'message', are active agents who construct their own sense of meaning from the music. The spectator or listener, as Rancière argues:

> observes, selects, compares, interprets. She links what she has seen to a host of things that she has seen on other stages, in other kinds of place. She composes her own poem with the elements of the poem before her.
>
> (2009, 13)

When listeners imagine meanings in response to the experience of music, they are, as Timmers suggests (2017, 489–90), among the several people who contribute to the process of musical communication. They are not merely an 'audience' who hear but do not participate in making the experience. I would describe the roles as follows:

1. A composer imagines musical ideas or a concept for a piece. These are likely to be analogous to senses or experiences of their own and to emerge in actual or imagined interaction with performers, instruments, and notation systems. They find these ideas please them and continue working on the piece in the same way.
2. Performers re-imagine the music from notation or imagine as they improvise, imagining as they engage with their instruments. With composed music, these imaginings will not be identical to those of the composer.
3. Listeners engage with the music in an embodied way and may perceive it as analogous to human experience. These perceptions will be unique to each listener since each has a different range of experience, though there is likely to be a convergence between meanings sensed in a piece of music by people from the same cultural group.
4. Any listener, whether composer, performer, or simply listener, may make semantic meanings from the musical experience to explain it to themselves or others.

Conclusion

Meaning making from music is the result of an act of imagination by the listener. This imaginative act is like the actions of inventing music when composing or performing since it arises from each person's subconscious dialogue activated by engagement with the society around. Musicians imagine in the context of their own experiences, and this results in music capable of being perceived as analogous to human experience. As Rancière puts it, they make '… a new sensory fabric by wresting percepts and affects from the perceptions and affections that made up the fabric of ordinary experience.' (2009, 56).

Any listener's perceptions of the music are then shaped both by their own understandings and the experience of the music. For the music to be experienced as meaningful in this way, it must be capable of provoking a sensory and embodied response which a listener feels to be analogous to human experience. Listeners who find themselves unable to engage in a specific piece are unlikely to experience it as meaningful. Music which lacks the quality of seeming analogous to human experience may not seem meaningful to listeners in general.

If a listener perceives a piece of music in this way, they may sometimes verbalise their sense. This appears to be linked to the way the more holistic perceptions felt in the right hemisphere tend to be summarised and interpreted in the left. These meanings will be constructed separately by each person, and so no one interpretation can be said to be definitive.

As with previous chapters, the view I suggest of the listening imagination draws on work by many other writers, from Langer through to Leman, Godøy, Clarke, Juslin, and several neuroscientists and other musicologists. I have re-expressed this view in terms of analogy perception and the distinction between experiential and semantic meaning and gone on to show that it relates to features of how the brain works. I also suggest that the processes are likely to be involuntary to some extent. If this view is accepted, then musical meanings will be made separately by each listener by applying their musical imagination to the experience of the music.

Notes

1 The argument presented in this chapter was first published in *Music & Practice*, Vol. VI, 2020; www.musicandpractice.org
2 Examples include: McClary (2004) on a Schubert Impromptu; Newcomb (1992) on Mahler's *9th Symphony*; Cone (1977) on a Brahms Intermezzo; Spitzer (1996) on Beethoven Piano Sonatas; Kramer (2002) on Schumann's *Carnaval*; McClary (1993) on Brahms' *3rd Symphony*; and Monahan (2007) and (2011) on Mahler's *6th and 7th Symphonies*.
3 See Ellis (2011) and Corballis (2014) who criticise these parts of McGilchrist's argument.

References

Albouy, Philippe, Lucas Benjamin, Benjamin Morillon, & Robert J. Zatorre. 2020. "Distinct Sensitivity to Spectrotemporal Modulation Supports Brain Asymmetry for Speech and Melody." *Science* 367 (6481): 1043–7. DOI: 10.1126/science.aaz3468

Bakhtin, Mikhail. 1981. *The Dialogic Imagination*. Translated by Caryl Emerson & Michael Holquist. Austin: University of Texas Press.

Barthes, Roland. 1977. "Death of the Author." In *Image Music Text*, by Roland Barthes, translated by Stephen Heath, 142–8. London: Fontana.

Beardsley, Monroe C. 1992. "The Authority of the Text." In *Intention and Interpretation*, edited by Gary Iseminger, 24–40. Philadelphia: Temple University Press.

Becker, Judith. 2004. *Deep Listeners: Music, Emotion, and Trancing.* Bloomington and Indianapolis: Indiana University Press.

———. 2011. "Exploring the Habitus of Listening: Anthropological Perspectives." In *Handbook of Music and Emotion: Theory, Research,*

Applications, edited by Patrik N. Juslin & John A. Sloboda, 127–57. Oxford & New York: Oxford University Press. DOI:10.1093/acprof:oso/9780199230143.001.0001
Bever, Thomas & Robert J. Chiarello. 1974. "Cerebral Dominance in Musicians and Non-Musicians." *Science* 185: 537–9.
Binder, Jeffrey R., Rutvik H. Desai, William W. Graves, & Lisa L. Conant. 2009. "Where is the Semantic System? A Critical Review and Meta-Analysis of 120 Functional Neuroscience-Imaging Studies." *Cerebral Cortex* 19: 2767–96. DOI: 10.1093/cercor/bhp055
Brattico, Elvira & Mari Tervaniemi. 2006. "Musical Creativity and the Human Brain." In *Musical Creativity: Multidisciplinary Research in Theory and Practice*, edited by Irène Deliège & Geraint Wiggins, 290–321. Hove & New York: Psychology Press.
Budd, Malcolm. 1985. *Music and Emotions*. London & New York: Routledge & Kegan Paul.
Burke, Sean. 2008. *The Death and Return of the Author*. Edinburgh: Edinburgh University Press.
Churchland, Patricia. 2011. *Braintrust*. Princeton, NJ: Princeton University Press.
Clarke, Eric F. 2005. *Ways of Listening: An Ecological Approach to the Perception of Musical Meaning*. Oxford & New York: Oxford University Press. DOI: 10.1093/acprof:oso/9780195151947.001.0001
Cone, Edward T. 1977. "Three Ways of Reading a Detective Story or a Brahms Intermezzo." *The Georgia Review* 31 (3): 283–6.
Cone, Edward T. 1985. "Beethoven's Orpheus – Or Janders?" *19th-Century Music* 8 (3): 283–6. DOI: 10.2307/746519
Cook, Nicholas. 2006. "Playing God: Creativity, Analysis, and Aesthetic Inclusion." In *Musical Creativity: Multidisciplinary Research in Theory and Practice*, edited by Irène Deliège & Geraint A. Wiggins, 9–24. Hove & New York: Psychology Press.
Corballis, Michael C. 2014. "Left Brain, Right Brain: Facts and Fantasies." *PLoS Biology* 12 (1). DOI: 10.1371/journal.pbio.1001767
Cox, Arnie. 2001. "The Mimetic Hypothesis and Embodied Musical Meaning." *Musicae Scientiae* 5 (2): 195–209. DOI: 10.1177/102986490100500204
———. 2011. "Embodying Music: Principles of the Mimetic Hypothesis." *Music Theory Online* 17 (2): No pagination. DOI: 10.30535/mto.17.2.1
Crispin, Darla & Stefan Östersjö. 2017. "Musical Expression from Conception to Reception." In *Musicians in the Making: Pathways to Creative Performance*, edited by John Rink, Helena Gaunt, & Aaron Williamon, 288–305. Oxford & New York: Oxford University Press. DOI:10.1093/acprof:oso/9780199346677.001.0001
Cross, Ian. 2009–10. "The Evolutionary Nature of Musical Meaning." *Musicae Scientiae* 13 (2): 179–200. DOI: 10.1177/1029864909013002091
Damasio, Antonio. 2006. *Descartes' Error: Emotion, Reason and the Human Brain*. London: Vintage Books.

Davies, Stephen. 2006. "Artistic Expression and the Hard Case of Pure Music." In *Contemporary Debates in Aesthetics and the Philosophy of Art*, edited by Matthew Kieran, 179–91. Malden MA & Oxford: Blackwell Publishing.

Deliège, Irène. 2006. "Analogy: Creative Support to Elaborate a Model of Musical Listening." In *Musical Creativity: Multidisciplinary Research in Theory and Practice*, edited by Irène Deliège & Geraint Wiggins, 63–77. Hove & New York: Psychology Press.

Delis, Dean, John Fleer, & Nancy H. Kerr. 1978. "Memory for Music." *Perception and Psychophysics* 23: 215–18. DOI: 10.3758/BF03204128

DeNora, Tia. 2000. *Music in Everyday Life*. Cambridge: Cambridge University Press. DOI: 10.1017/CBO9780511489433

Derrida, Jacques. 1976. *Of Grammatology*. Translated by Gayatri Chakravotri Spivak. Baltimore and London: The Johns Hopkins University Press.

Downey, June E. 1897. "A Musical Experiment." *The American Journal of Psychology* 9 (1): 63–9.

Ellis, Robert M. 2011. "Extended Review of 'The Master and his Emissary' by Iain McGilchrist." *Middle Way Society* 11. Accessed 26 October 2018. www.middlewaysociety.org/books/psychology-books/the-master-and-his-emissary-by-iain-mcgilchrist/

Fontaine, Sheryl I. & Susan M. Hunter. 2006. *Collaborative Writing in Composition Studies*. Boston MA and London: Thomson Wadsworth.

Foucault, Michel. 1979. *What is an Author?* Accessed 11 November 2015. www.open.edu/openlearn/ocw/pluginfile.php/624849/mod_resource/content/1/a840_1_michel_foucault.pdf

Gabrielsson, Alf. 2011. Strong Experiences with Music: Music is Much More Than Just Music. Oxford & New York: Oxford University Press. DOI:10.1093/acprof:oso/9780199695225.001.0001

———. 2011a. "Strong Experiences with Music." In Handbook of Music and Emotion: Theory, Research, Applications, edited by Patrik N. Juslin & John A. Sloboda, 547–74. Oxford & New York: Oxford University Press. DOI:10.1093/acprof:oso/9780199230143.001.0001

Gadamer, Hans-Georg. 1997. *Philosophical Hermeneutics*. Translated by D.E. Linge. Berkley and Los Angeles: University of California Press.

Gallese, Vittorio, Luciano Fadiga, Leonardo Fogassi, & Giacomo Rizzolatti. 1996. "Action Recognition in the Premotor Cortex." *Brain* 19: 593–609. www.researchgate.net/publication/285797377_Action_recognition_in_the_premotor_cortex

Gallese, Vittorio & Alvin Goldman. 1998. "Mirror Neurons and the Simulation Theory of Mind-Reading." *Trends in Cognitive Science* 12 (2): 493–501. DOI: 10.1016/S1364-6613(98)01262-5

Gallese, Vittorio. 2008. "Mirror Neurons and the Neural Exploitation Hypothesis: From Embodied Simulation to Social Cognition." In *Mirror Neuron Systems. Contemporary Neuroscience*, edited by Jaime A. Pineda, 163–90. New York: Humana Press.

———. 2009. "Mirror Neurons, Embodied Simulation and the Neural Basis of Social Identification." *Psychoanalytic Dialogues* 19 (5): 519–36. DOI: 10.1080/10481880903231910

Gaut, Berys & Paisley Livingston. 2003. "Introduction: The Creation of Art: Issues and Perspectives." In *The Creation of Art*, edited by Berys Gaut & Paisley Livingston, 1–32. Cambridge & New York: Cambridge University Press.

Gazzaniga, Michael S. 1998. "The Split Brain Revisited." *Scientific American* 279 (1): 50–5. DOI: 10.1038/scientificamerican0798-50

Gentner, Dedre. 1989. "The Mechanisms of Analogical Learning." In *Similarity and Analogical Reasoning*, edited by Stella Vosniadou & Andrew Ortony, 199–241. Cambridge & New York: Cambridge University Press. DOI: 10.1017/CBO9780511529863

Gibson, James J. 1986. *The Ecological Approach to Visual Perception*. Hillsdale NJ: Lawrence Erlbaum Associates.

Godøy, Rolf I. 2010. "Gestural Affordances of Musical Sound." In *Musical Gestures: Sound, Movement, and Meaning*, edited by Rolf I. Godøy, & Marc Leman, 103–25. New York & Abingdon: Routledge.

Hargreaves, David J., James J. Hargreaves, & Adrian C. North. 2012. "Imagination and Creativity in Listening." In *Musical Imaginations: Multidisciplinary Perspectives on Creativity, Performance, and Perception*, edited by David J. Hargreaves, Dorothy E. Miell & Raymond A.R. MacDonald, 156–72. Oxford: Oxford University Press. DOI: 10.1093/acprof:oso/9780199568086.001.0001

Harkaway, Nick. 2017. "I Have a Firework Going Off in My Head and I Have to Describe It." *The Guardian Review* 11 (11): 11. www.theguardian.com/books/2017/nov/11/nick-harkaway-gnomon-interview

Hickok, Gregory. 2009. "Eight Problems for the Mirror Neuron Theory of Action Understanding in Monkeys and Humans." *Journal of Cognitive Neuroscience* 21 (7): 1229–43. DOI: 10.1162/jocn.2009.21189

———. 2014. *The Myth of Mirror Neurons: The Real Neuroscience of Communication and Cognition*. New York & London: W.W Norton & Co.

Hirsch, Eric D. Jnr. 1992. "In Defense of the Author." In *Intention and Interpretation*, edited by Gary Iseminger, 11–23. Philadelphia: Temple University Press.

Horace. 2000. "The Art of Poetry." In *Classical Literary Criticism*, translated by Penelope Murray & T.S. Dorsch, 98–112. London: Penguin Books.

Jackendoff, Ray & Fred Lerdahl. 2006. "The Capacity for Music: What Is It and What's Special About It?" *Cognition* 100 (1): 33–72. www.researchgate.net/publication/279235446_The_capacity_for_music_what_is_it_and_what%27s_special_about_it

Jander, Owen. 1985. "Beethoven's 'Orpheus in Hades': The 'Andante Con Moto' of the Fourth Piano Concerto." *19th-Century Music* 8 (3): 195–212. DOI: 10.4324/9781315096506-21

Jander, Owen. 1999. "Orpheus Revisited: A Ten-Year Retrospective on the Andante con moto of Beethoven's Fourth Piano Concerto." *19th-Century Music* 19 (1): 31–49. DOI: 10.1525/ncm.1995.19.1.02a00020

Juslin, Patrick N., Simon Liljeström, Daniel Västfjäll, & Lars-Olov Lundqvist. 2011. "How Does Music Evoke Emotions? Exploring the Underlying Mechanisms." In *Handbook of Music and Emotion: Theory, Research, Applications*, edited by Patrik N. Juslin & John A. Sloboda, 605–42. Oxford & New York: Oxford University Press. DOI:10.1093/acprof:oso/9780199230143.001.0001

Juslin, Patrick N. 2019. *"Musical Emotions Explained: Unlocking the Secrets of Musical Affect."* Oxford: Oxford University Press. DOI:10.1093/oso/9780198753421.001.0001

Kerman, Joseph. 1992. "Representing a Relationship: Notes on a Beethoven Concerto." *Representations* 39 (Summer): 80–101. DOI: 10.1525/rep.1992.39.1.99p0125c

Kramer, Lawrence. 2002. "Rethinking Schumann's Carnaval: Identity, Meaning, and the Social Order." In *Musical Meaning: Toward a Critical History*, edited by Lawrence Kramer, 100–32. Berkeley: University of California Press.

Langer, Susanne K. 1942. *Philosophy in a New Key*. Cambridge: Cambridge University Press.

Leech-Wilkinson, Daniel. 2012. "Compositions, Scores, Performances, Meanings." *Music Theory Online* 18 (1). Accessed 7 June 2018. mtosmt.org/issues/mto.12.18.1/mto.12.18.1.leech-wilkinson.php DOI: 10.2307/843535

Leman, Marc. 2008. *Embodied Music Cognition and Mediation Technology*. Cambridge MA: The MIT Press.

———. 2010. "Music, Gesture, and the Formation of Embodied Meaning." In *Musical Gestures: Sound, Movement, and Meaning*, edited by Rolf I. Godøy & Marc Leman, 126–53. New York & Abingdon: Routledge

Lerdahl, Fred, & Ray Jackendoff. 1983. *A Generative Theory of Tonal Music*. Cambridge MA: The MIT Press.

Levinson, Jerrold. 1992. "Intention and Interpretation: A Last Look." In *Intention and Interpretation*, edited by Gary Iseminger, 221–56. Philadelphia: Temple University Press.

Lilienfeld, Scott O., Steven Jay Lynn, John Ruscio, & Barry L. Beyerstein. 2010. *50 Great Myths of Popular Psychology*. Chichester and Maldon MA: Wiley-Blackwell.

Lingnau, A., B. Gesierich, & A. Caramazza. 2009. "Asymmetric fMRI Adaptation Reveals No Evidence for Mirror Neurons in Humans." *Proceedings of the National Academy of Sciences* 106 (24): 9925–30. DOI: 10.1073/pnas.0902262106

Livingston, Paisley. 2005. *Art and Intention: A Philosophical Study*. Oxford: Clarendon Press.

Lotze, Martin, Gabriela Sheler, & Nils Birbaumer. 2006. "From Music Perception to Creative Performance: Mapping Cerebral Differences Between Professional and Amateur Musicians." In *Musical Creativity: Multidisciplinary Research in Theory and Practice*, edited by Irène Deliège & Geraint Wiggins, 275–89. Hove & New York: Psychology Press.

Marsh, Diane T. & Judith Vollmer. 1991. "The Polyphonic Creative Process: Experiences of Artists and Writers." *Journal of Creative Behaviour* 25 (2): 106–15. DOI: 10.1002/j.2162-6057.1991.tb01360.x

Maus, Fred E. 2005. "Classical Instrumental Music and Narrative." In *A Companion to Narrative Theory*, edited by James Phelan & Peter J. Rabinowitz, 466–83. Malden MA & Oxford: Blackwell Publishing.

McClary, Susan. 1993. "Narrative Agendas in "Absolute Music": Identity and Difference in Brahms's Third Symphony." In *Musicology and Difference*, edited by R.A. Solie, 326–44. Berkeley, CA.
McClary, Susan. 2004. "The Impromptu Which Stood on a Loaf." In *Narrative Theory: Critical Concepts in Cultural Studies*, edited by Mieke Bal, 20–35. London: Routledge.
McGilchrist, Iain. 2009. *The Master and his Emissary: The Divided Brain and the Making of the Western World*. New Haven & London: Yale University Press.
Mendelssohn Bartholdy, P. & C. Mendelssohn Bartholdy. 2001. *Letters of Felix Mendelssohn Bartholdy from 1833–1847*. Boston, MA: Elibron Classics, Adamant Media Corporation.
Merleau-Ponty, Maurice. 2014. *The Phenomenology of Perception*. Translated by Donald A. Landes. Abingdon: Routledge.
Metcalfe, Janet, Margaret Funnell, & Michael S. Gazzaniga. 1995. "Right-Hemisphere Memory Superiority: Studies of a Split-Brain Patient." *Psychological Science* 6 (3): 157–64. DOI: 10.1111/j.1467-9280.1995.tb00325.x
Molnar-Szakacs, Istvan, Vanya Green Assuied, & Kate Overy. 2012. "Shared Affective Motion Experience (SAME) and Creative, Interactive Music Therapy." In *Musical Imaginations: Multidisciplinary Perspectives on Creativity, Performance, and Perception*, edited by David J. Hargreaves, Dorothy E. Miell & Raymond A.R. MacDonald, 313–31. Oxford: Oxford University Press. DOI: 10.1093/acprof:oso/9780199568086.001.0001
Monahan, Seth. 2007. "'Inescapable' Coherence and the Failure of the Novel-Symphony in the Finale of Mahler's Sixth." *19th-Century Music* 31 (1): 53–95. DOI: 10.1525/ncm.2007.31.1.053
———. 2011. "Success and Failure in Mahler's Sonata Recapitulations." *Music Theory Spectrum* 33 (1): 37–58. DOI: 10.1525/mts.2011.33.1.37
Nattiez, Jean-Jaques. 1990. "Can One Speak of Narrativity in Music?" *Journal of the Royal Musical Association* 115: 240–57. DOI: 10.1093/jrma/115.2.240
Newcomb, Anthony. 1992. "Narrative Archetypes and Mahler's Ninth Symphony." In *Music and Text: Critical Inquiries*, edited by Stephen Paul Scher, 118–36. Cambridge & New York: Cambridge University Press.
Novick, Laura R. 1988. "Analogical Transfer, Problem Similarity, and Expertise." *Journal of Experimental Psychology: Learning, Memory, and Cognition* 14 (3): 510–20. DOI: 10.1037//0278-7393.14.3.510
Patel, Aniruddh D. 2008. *Music, Language, and the Brain*. Oxford University Press.
Pinker, Stephen. 1997. *How the Mind Works*. London & New York: Penguin Books.
Plato. 2016. *Apology: The Apology of Socrates*. Cabin John MD: Wildside Press.
Rancière, Jacques. 2009. *The Emancipated Spectator*. Translated by Gregory Elliott. London & New York: Verso.
Reybrouck, Mark M. 2006. "Musical Creativity Between Symbolic Modelling and Perceptual Constraints: The Role of Adaptive Behaviour and Epistemic

Autonomy." In *Musical Creativity: Multidisciplinary Research in Theory and Practice*, edited by Irène Deliège & Geraint A. Wiggins, 42–59. Hove & New York: Psychology Press.

Rizzolatti, Giacomo, Leonardo Fogassi, & Vittorio Gallese. 2001. "Neurophysiological Mechanisms Underlying the Understanding and Imitation of Action." *Nature Reviews: Neuroscience* 2 (9): 661–70. DOI: 10.1038/35090060

Schütz, Alfred. 1951. "Making Music Together: A Study in Social Relationship." *Social Research* 18 (1): 76–97.

Spitzer, Michael. 1996. "Narratives of Self-Consciousness in Proust and Beethoven." In *Musical Semiotics in Growth*, edited by Eero Tarasti, 329–45. Bloomington: Indiana University Press.

Tagg, Philip. 2013. *Music's Meanings: A Modern Musicology for Non-Musos*. Larchmont NY: The Mass Media Music Scholars' Press.

Taylor, Alan. 2020. "Death of the Composer? Meaning Making from Musical Performance." *Music & Practice* 6: Unpaginated. DOI: 10.32063/0605

Thompson, William F. 2015. *Music, Thought, and Feeling: Understanding the Psychology of Music*. New York & Oxford: Oxford University Press.

Timmers, Renee. 2017. "Emotion in Music Listening." In *The Routledge Companion to Music Cognition*, edited by Richard Ashley & Renee Timmers, 489–98. New York and Abingdon: Routledge.

Toolan, Michael. 2011. "La Narrativité Musicale." *Cahiers de Narratologie* 21 (3): 1–10. DOI: 10.4000/narratologie.6489

Umilta, M.A., E. Kohler, V. Gallese, L. Fogassi, L. Fadiga, & C. Keysers. 2001. "I Know What You Are Doing: A Neurophysiological Study." *Neuron* 31: 155–65. DOI: 10.1016/S0896-6273(01)00337-3

Vosniadou, Stella & Andrew Ortony. 1989. *Similarity and Analogical Reasoning*. Cambridge & New Rochelle: Cambridge University Press. DOI: 10.1017/CBO9780511529863

Wimsatt, William K. & Monroe C. Beardsley. 1954. "The Intentional Fallacy." In *The Verbal Icon: Studies in the Meaning of Poetry*, edited by William K. Wimsatt, 3–20. Lexington: University of Kentucky Press.

Wolford, George, Michael Miller, & Michael S. Gazzaniga. 2000. "The Left Hemisphere's Role in Hypothesis Formation." *Journal of Neuroscience* 20 (6): 1–4. DOI: 10.1523/JNEUROSCI.20-06-j0003.2000

Zatorre, Robert J. & Pascal Belin. 2001. "Spectral and Temporal Processing in Human Auditory Cortex." *Cerebral Cortex* 949–53. DOI: 10.1093/cercor/11.10.946

Zbikowski, Lawrence M. 2017. "Music, Analogy, and Metaphor." In *The Routledge Companion to Music Cognition*, edited by Richard Ashley & Renee Timmers, 501–12. New York & Abingdon: Routledge.

A final word

The conclusions reached at the end of each of my main chapters need no further elaboration, though it is worth summarising them here before going on to discuss three implications of the way I suggest the musical imagination works, two of which I touched on earlier.

I argued that musical imagination is not limited to a small number of exceptional people who are able to produce music just from their own minds but is an ability we all possess. Our musical ideas or understandings arise from the varied experiences which enter into dialogue in our subconscious minds, resulting in ideas popping into consciousness as if from nowhere. The fact that the musical imagination is rooted in the subconscious is bound to constrain the ability of musicians to share their imaginative processes with other artists when they work together. These constraints mean that they will find they can work together in a number of distinct and definable ways. Another consequence of musical ideas arising from a subconscious dialogue is that they will be inherently complex and ambiguous. Musical meanings therefore cannot be said to be communicated directly by musicians to listeners. Rather, listeners use their own imaginations to make meanings from their individual experiences of music as long as they can perceive it as analogous to human experience.

The **first** implication on which it is worth expanding is that musical imagination must be a universal ability. There can be no such thing as a person lacking this ability unless some mental or physiological limitation prevents them from being so. Music, after all, is universal throughout human cultures. It developed early in the evolution of modern humans and is thought to have played an important role in consolidating their small and insecure social groups. Evidence of this early development of music is presented by writers such as Mithen (2005), Tomlinson (2015), and many others. Probably everyone above a certain age took part as they do in tribal music such as that documented by Blacking (1971).

If the ability to make music is universal, then no-one should be inhibited by the brilliance of top musical practitioners. Yes, some people seem to have a greater level of musical ability than others, and the same could be said of any skill. Even so, engagement in music should be seen as a normal human activity, not the preserve of professionals. If people find personal satisfaction and a sense of meaning from making music with others, then that is a sufficient justification in itself. As Sontag suggests of literature, music is '... one of the resources we have for helping us to make sense of our lives ...' (2007, 221).

That leads to the **second** implication. Since the musical imagination is not a mysterious quality, but something we understand to a fair extent, it follows that we can learn to use it more effectively. Listening skill can be developed to a higher level through practice, as can compositional and performance skill. Anyone can start a new musical activity and work to improve. As skilled musicians testify, their high level of skill is mainly the result of a great deal of effective practice.

Highly imaginative people often have that quality because they were encouraged when young and, importantly, they were not discouraged as they grew. I quoted Picasso's view that every child is an artist (2016). Every adult must then be capable of being an artist, but unfortunately in our society that may mean re-learning the freedom of spirit which will too often have been discouraged earlier in life. It is worth trying to regain this ability since imaginative and creative activity contribute to the sense of being a complete human being.

There is a **third** implication, which results from the view that music and musical understandings result from our engagement in society and our environment. Musical ideas come from all we have absorbed and are a remaking of our experiences. Ideas for a new piece, a way of performing, or an understanding of a piece of music, are not just our own but are perceptions derived from our environments filtered through our individual imaginations. As a result, artists have a choice and both options are, in a sense, political.

One option is to assert that one's art, or perception of art, is 'unpolitical' and separate from the society around. The first problem with this attitude is that it involves a denial of the evidence that art is imagined as a result of engagement with our society and environment. The second is that the assertion that art should be free from 'political' implications is itself a political view that art should not affect the society around, and so not disturb the status quo. As George Orwell put it, '... the opinion that art should have nothing to do with politics is itself a political attitude.' (2019).

A final word

The alternative is to accept the inevitability of one's relationship to society. When an artist imagines they remake aspects of their experience of society, and their art may have an effect on that society. If they consciously accept this reciprocal relationship, they should also accept that they have a responsibility as actors in that society. As Ai Weiwei puts it, 'An artist must also be an activist.' (2020, 13).

This is the concept of artistic citizenship, explored in a set of essays edited by Elliott, Silverman, and Bowman (2016). Their argument is that artists should open themselves to the world around and engage actively in that world, welcoming these influences into their art, imagining on the assumption that they will be sensing and experiencing on behalf of their community.

The obvious risk for any socially engaged artist is being led to make art intended as an intervention in, or comment on, societal issues. It will be more productive and effective, as Ai Weiwei puts it, to '… deal with these issues through artistic language.' (2020, 11). Art needs to be allowed to arise from subconscious rumination on societal experience. Rather than seeking to intervene directly, it is better to engage in society and then allow the imagination to produce what it will. Social engagement of this type by an artist amounts to an act of resistance to the pressure we currently face to conform to the prevailing neo-liberal ideology which, as Mould (2018) and Cook (2018, 197) argue, seeks to frame artists as lone creators competing, and encourages the production of novelties of no significance.

I quoted Rancière (2009) in Chapter 4, and his book was in part written in response to the analysis by Guy Debord in *The Society of Spectacle* (1967) of how modern capitalism seeks to reduce people to passivity by engaging them in meaningless spectacles such as celebrity culture. Rancière's view is that we can emancipate ourselves from the control of the spectacles Debord describes since the true nature of perception is that we make our own meanings from experience. Social engagement by an artist can contribute to this emancipation, and so act as a form of resistance to neo-liberal ideology. As Bernstein puts it 'Art cannot change events. But it can change people. It can affect people so that they are changed … because people are changed by art – enriched, ennobled, encouraged – they then act in a way that may affect the course of events …' (2018).

While there is nothing new in this argument, I am making one new suggestion, that whether to let their experience of the world around them come through in their art is not really a matter of choice for an artist. I presented a view of how the imagination works, that we absorb external influences which are then in dialogue in our subconscious minds, and art may emerge. The art will then, inevitably, be affected by the artist's engagement in their society since that is how their imagination works. There is no other option.

The choice which is open to artists is not whether to imagine in a social context, but whether consciously to open themselves to this engagement and aim to maximise it, or to seek to minimise its impact on their art. I suggest that the first option will be the better choice since the art will then be more likely to engage audiences. If art is analogous to societal experience to the fullest possible extent, then audiences are more likely to respond and make meanings from the experience.

Whichever choice an artist makes, my argument remains that societal engagement by artists is not voluntary. Artists and their audiences cannot escape remaking social experience as they imagine, since that appears to be how their imaginations work.

References

Bernstein, Leonard. 2018. *Leonard Bernstein Quotes.* Accessed 10 March 2020. www.goodreads.com/quotes/8747636-the-point-is-art-never-stopped-a-war-and-never.

Blacking, John. 1971. *How Musical is Man?* Seattle and London: University of Washington Press. DOI: 10.21504/amj.v5i3.1669

Cook, Nicholas. 2018. *Music as Creative Practice.* Oxford: Oxford University Press. DOI: 10.1093/oso/9780199347803.001.0001

Debord, Guy. 1967. "Society of the Spectacle." Accessed 03 March 2010. www.marxists.org/reference/archive/debord/society.htm

Elliot, David J., Marissa Silverman, & Wayne D. Bowman. 2016. *Artistic Citizenship: Artistry, Social Responsibility, and Ethical Praxis.* Oxford and New York: Oxford University Press. DOI: 10.1093/acprof:oso/9780199393749.001.0001

Mithen, Stephen. 2005. *The Singing Neanderthals: The Origins of Music, Language, Mind, and Body.* London: Weidenfeld and Nicholson. DOI: 10.1017/S0959774306000060

Mould, Oli. 2018. *Against Creativity.* London and New York: Verso.

Orwell, George. 2019. *AZquotes: George Orwell Quotes.* Accessed 26 January 2020. www.azquotes.com/author/11147-George_Orwell/tag/attitude

Picasso, Pablo. 2016. "Pablo Picasso Quotes." *BrainyQuote.* Accessed 19 July 2018. www.brainyquote.com/quotes/pablo_picasso_104106

Rancière, Jacques. 2009. *The Emancipated Spectator.* Translated by Gregory Elliott. London & New York: Verso.

Sontag, Susan. 2007. *At the Same Time.* London and New York: Penguin Books.

Tomlinson, Gary. 2015. *A Million Years of Music: The Emergence of Human Modernity*. New York: Zone Books (MIT Press). mitpress.mit.edu/books/million-years-music

Weiwei, Ai. 2020. "Interview." *The Observer* 3 (22): 10–13. www.theguardian.com/artanddesign/2020/jan/21/ai-weiwei-on-his-new-life-in-britain-germany-virtual-reality-film

Index

Actor-Network Theory 32
Adams, John 54, 57–8
ambiguity in art 25, 26, 28, 39, 78, 79, 107
analogy: communication by 88; perception through 90
art world 7
Auerbach, Frank 2

Bach, J. C. 13
Bach, J. S.: as a German composer 9; and musical works 12
Bakhtin, Mikhail 27–9, 94
Barthes, Roland 78, 94; *Death of the Author* 78, 80
Beethoven: ideas arriving unbidden 41, 42; *Piano Concerto No. 4* 83–4; and sketching 8, 45; taking walks 36; as unfettered genius 12, 13, 19
Bernstein, Leonard 109
bodily perception: integration into mind 37–9, 88–9, 93
brain: activity during sleep 37; areas and subconscious 18–19, 35; as computer 31; integration of bodily sensing 37–9, 89
brain areas: conceptual/semantic 94; motor/sensory 94
brain hemispheres: forms of perception 96–7; left and analytic processing 97–8; music and language 96; myths 96; right and holistic processing 97–8

Britten, Benjamin: and walking or taking a break 36
Brontës 56

Cage, John 57, 64
Centre for Musical Performance as Creative Practice (CMPCP) 10–11
cheesecake, auditory 76
Chopin, Frédéric 15
co-operation 58–60, 64–5, 71; forms of 61
cognition: and analogies 92; embodied 37, 89, 94
collaboration 3, 54–5; alternative forms of 58; experience of 66–7; with non-human third parties 55; performer studies of 17, 63; tighter definition of 58–9
concert halls: public 13; silent audience in 85
consultation 58, 60, 62
Copland, Aaron 41; *Appalachian Spring* 63–4
copyright of music 13–14
craftspeople, composers as 13
creativity: ideology of 17–18; and neoliberalism 18, 20, 109; in art 8; imagination and 2; non-conscious 34; research on 10
creativity, distributed 6, 7, 9–11, 15, 39, 57, 70
Cunningham, Merce 57, 64

Descartes, René 30, and the soul and body 37

Index

dialogic: art 27, 28; imagination 27–9, 37; inner voice 34; process in composition 28; self 27, 28
Dukas, Paul; L'Apprenti Sorcier 83

embodied engagement 3, 88–9, 92–3, 95
embodied music perception 38, 89, 92; and brain areas 95
Empson, William 25

genius: composer as 3, 6–9, 11; and collaboration 17; as creators of musical works 15; as gender stereotype 17; as ideology 16; as myth 6, 16; solitary or lone 2, 6, 12, 17
Gluck, Christof von 36
gut feeling: and still small voice 37

Handel: *The Messiah* 70; oboe concertos 70
Helmholtz, Herman von 36
hierarchical working 60, 65
Hindemith, Paul: and Massine 64–5
Horace 96
Housman, A. E. 42, 77

imagining: embodied 37; as individual process 11; in medium of the art 43–4, 48
impressionists 56
inner voice or speech 26, 34, 54, 67; dialogic 27, 34; Socrates 27
intentionalism 77–9

James, Henry 45
James, William 27
jazz improvisation 54, 55, 57, 66, 67

Latour, Bruno 32
learning: emotion-guided 31, 33; imaginative 29–30
Lennon and McCartney 56
listening, habitus of 85
Liszt, Franz 15

Mahler, Gustav: Symphony No. 6 14; taking walks 36

meaning: shared creation of 67
Mendelssohn, Felix 85
mirror neurons: and action understanding 92; and analogies 92–5
Mozart: and freemasonry 9; and musical work concept 13; operatic arias 70; playing billiards 42; source of ideas 42; and walking 36
music: cultural universality of 107; early evolution of 107
musical meaning: and previous experience 94–5; verbalisation of 95; verbalisation and brain hemispheres 97–8
musical work: as ideology 16; as regulative concept 16

neoliberal ideology 109
neurological processes: in imagining 18; in music listening 91

Ode to Joy 8, 45
Orwell, George 108

Picasso, Pablo 18, 58, 108
Pinter, Harold 42–3, 45–6, 67
Poincaré, Henri 34–6, 38
pop song writing 54, 69, 70

recalled experience: reliability of 35–6, 40
Rossini, Gioachino: and taking a break 36

Saariaho, Kaija 43
Schoenberg, Arnold 8
school composition projects 69
Schubert, Franz 14–15
Sessions, Roger 42
shared voice 67
Sillitoe, Alan 42
Socrates 27, 75
still small voice 27, 37
Stockhausen, Karlheinz: finding ideas after sleep 36–7
Strauss, Richard 36, 42; and Massine 65; and taking a break 36, 42

Stravinsky, Igor: and Balanchine 58
subconscious thought or dialogue 3, 4, 18, 19, 25, 28, 33–7, 43, 54, 109; active while distracted 36; challenged by Perkins 35–6; embodied 38–9; sense of rightness 38, 46

Taverner, John 41, 45
Tchaikovsky, Pyotr 41
12-tone series 8

Vygotsky, Lev 29–30, 33

Weiwei, Ai 109
Western Art Music 2, 6, 12, 16, 68

For Product Safety Concerns and Information please contact our EU representative GPSR@taylorandfrancis.com
Taylor & Francis Verlag GmbH, Kaufingerstraße 24, 80331 München, Germany

www.ingramcontent.com/pod-product-compliance
Lightning Source LLC
Chambersburg PA
CBHW070739230426
43669CB00014B/2518